CHRISTIANITY AND BUDDHISM

COMPARED

CHRISTIANITY AND BUDDHISM

COMPARED

REV. R. SPENCE HARDY

GYAN

Published by

GYAN

Gyan Publishing House
5, Ansari Road
Daryaganj, New Delhi-110002
Phone: 011-47034999, 9811692060
E-mail: books@gyanbooks.com

Distribution Network
gyanbooks.com
India, USA, Canada, UK, Australia, France

ISBN: 978-81-212-9430-0 (PB)
First Published, 1874

2nd Impression 2023

Printed at: Gyan Press, Delhi.

CHRISTIANITY AND BUDDHISM

AUTHOR: R. SPENCE HARDY

CHRISTIANITY AND BUDDHISM

COMPARED.

BY THE LATE

REV. R. SPENCE HARDY,

HON. MEM. ROYAL ASIATIC SCCIETY.

COLOMBO:

WESLEYAN MISSION PRESS.

MDCCCLXXIV.

THE following work is the last production of the Author. The earlier portion was carefully revised by him, and as few corrections as possible have been made in the text of the remaining chapters. Probably, a final contrast between "the life eternal" of the Christian's hope and the *Nirwána* of the Buddhist writings would have been added, had the life of the veteran missionary been spared.

Colombo, November 16th, 1874.

INDEX.

INTRODUCTION.

The last of the five essential properties of Existence, according to the Buddhists, is Discrimination, one quality of which is, "the power of producing thought from similarity, or resemblance"; as, when a man sees one of his fellow-men, he is reminded thereby of his own father, or of some other relative; from seeing a camel, a bull, or an ass, he is reminded of other camels, bulls, or asses, and of the characteristics of each: and from seeing a numeral, he is reminded of other numerals, and of their relative proportions. This institution of parallelisms between objects of similar character has something in it so accordant with the mental processes of every day life, that we can scarcely look at any product, or have brought before us any system, in relation to which, on a study of its properties or principles, they are not at once perceived; and in proportion to the importance of the objects upon which the mind dwells, and their nearness to each other, in figure or attribute, must be the interest of the investigation.

We now propose to institute an enquiry into some of the principal resemblances and contrarieties between Christianity and Buddhism; believing that by this mode of quest the supremacy of Christianity will be the more firmly established, and a clearer insight will be gained into the dogmas said to have been taught by Sákya Muni. The work is written for this one purpose. It is not extended as a formal defence of the doctrines of revelation: nor does it profess to present either a full account of the history of Buddhism, or a systematic exposition of its tenets.

There is, however, so much that is striking in the legendary history of Sákya Muni, and so much that is excellent in the code of morals attributed to him—the system he established spread so rapidly and widely, and it is at the present moment received by so many millions of the human race,—that by many powerful reasons we are called upon to attempt an examination of the Buddhist records that have come down to us, in order that we may learn therefrom what were the sources whence his system was derived, and some account of his life. But we are met, at the beginning of our researches, by keen disappointment: as the information we possess concerning them, upon which we can implicitly rely, is provokingly scanty. The deeds and doctrines of no teacher who has appeared upon earth have been more minutely recorded; but they are so much mixed up with tedious details of things absurd or impossible, that an attempt to separate the trustworthy from the fanciful, would be like the search for a handful of pearls amidst a shell-mound high as the monumental towers erected in various places over the relics of his disciples.

Modern research has discovered that there are two great schools of Buddhism, which, from the want of a more distinctive designation, are known by the names of Northern and Southern. The original works belonging to the former division are principally in Sanskrit, and those to the latter in Páli. It is thought by many of the best European orientalists that we have not yet sufficient data to decide which class is the more ancient, or possessed of the greater authority; but among the Buddhists themselves each section claims precedence for the particular language used in its own religious observances.

The first European who set himself seriously to the study of the system was Mr. Brian Haughton Hodgson, who was appointed, in 1841, to an official position in Nepaul, by the East India Government. In this situation he had great facilities for translating a number of works he there met with, written in the Sanskrit language. Soon afterwards, M. Alexander Csoma Körösi, a native of Transylvania, penetrated into Tibet, subjecting himself to many hardships, and nobly persevering amidst the most formidable difficulties, until he had studied the principal works in its literature, consisting of several hundreds of volumes. An abstract of his researches was published in the Bengal Asiatic Journal, when it was found that the Nepaulese and Tibetan works are derived from the same source. The Buddhist literature of China, said to be so vast as almost to defy an estimate of its extent, has elements agreeing with both the schools, and some additions of indigenous origin. In the rich mine of Buddhism there have been many laborious workers who are thus enumerated by Max Müller: " Hodgson, Turnour, Csoma de Körösi, S. Julien,

Fonceaux, Fausböll, Spence Hardy, and above all the late Eugene Burnouf": to which may be added, the names of Gogerly and Brigandet. In 183– the Hon. George Turnour, of the Ceylon Civil Service, commenced a series of papers in the Bengal Asiatic Journal, on the Páli Annals of the Buddhists: and afterwards published separately a translation from Páli of the first thirty-eight chapters of the Mahawanso, the most important historical work yet discovered in India: in which there is a mass of error, but containing also a few fragments of valuable truth. The Rev. Daniel John Gogerly, of the Wesleyan Mission, who died at Colombo, in 1862, brought a mind of great metaphysical power to the study of the sacred books in their original language, but he has left behind him little more than a few essays and translations, precious as dust of gold, published principally in a small local periodical, called the Friend, and in the Journal of the Ceylon Branch of the Royal Asiatic Society, 1845—61.

The most authentic sources of the information we derive from the Páli are the Tripitaka. These works are regarded by the Buddhists, as a record of pure unmixed truth, without any deposit of error, or possibility of mistake. We are not aware that any attempt has been made to form an analysis of their contents, beyond a meagre enumeration of the titles of the principle divisions, and an estimate of the length to which they extend. A few of the more important discourses of Buddha have been translated, and excerpts from others have made on particular subjects. The greater part of the Buddhist lore that has hitherto been made accessible to European readers, has come to us mediately from Mongolia, Tibet, Nepaul, Burma, Siam, China, and Ceylon: in all which countries the system is still professed, as well as in Kashmire, Tartary, and Annam. The legends they present have a wonderful agreement with each other, but in their dogmas there is a more marked diversity of thought and character. We may not be able, from these materials, to discover what was the full form of original Buddhism, but they are of interest, as shewing the effects of the system on different minds, and among nations of varied races.*

---

* Were Italian popery, English puritanism, and German rationalism given, to find apostolic Christianity, the problem would be like that of determining primitive Buddhism from its phases in Ceylon, Tibet, and Eastern India. It were as easy, from the present fauna and flora of the earth to determine its fauna and flora in the cretaceous, volitic, or caboniferous age. F. W. Mason, M. D. art. Mulamuli, Journal of the American Oriental Society, iv. 103.

The general indifference with which researches in Buddhism have been regarded, more especially in Britain, is difficult to account for; as, irrespective of the importance of the subject from its extent and influence, there are other matters of special interest connected with it, arising from the magnitude and antiquity of its architectural remains; its numerous inscriptions, upon coins, slabs and rocks, the key to the reading of which presents one of the most ingenious discoveries of modern study; the coincidence in some of its historical events with western chronology; and the light it throws upon a type of speculation differing widely from that which is seen in the systems and philosophies of the Semitic and European nations.

In our initial attempt to give an insight into the mysteries of the eastern grove, with its fragrance, brightly tinted flowers, and grateful shade, we shall first ask of the grave men who there dwelt, what are the the authorities upon which they rest their faith, and what are the reasons they adduce for maintaining that they are an unerring guide to the path of purity and the possession of peace.

BOOK I.

PREFATORY.

CHAPTER I.

THE RULE OF FAITH.

I. THE SCRIPTURES. II. THE TRIPITAKA. III. INSPIRATION OF THE SCRIPTURES. IV. SOURCE OF THE PITAKAS. V. CHRISTIAN TRADITION. VI. BUDDHIST TRADITION.

I. THE SCRIPTURES.

In the Church of Christ, the Scriptures of the prophets and apostles, and other "holy men of God," who "spake as they were moved by the Holy Ghost," form the standard of truth. Respecting the nature of their inspiration, its authority, its extent, and other questions of a similar character, there have been numberless controversies, each of which would require volumes for its full elucidation. We must pass by these with brief remarks, but shall be obliged in consequence to appear dogmatical, when, to some minds, it might have been more satisfactory if we had pursued a more apologetic course.

Appeal is made for the authority of the Scriptures to the supernatural effects wrought out by their writers, or by the agents through whom their principal truths were established, and to the prophecies they contain as to the events of the future. The New Testament was written by men who had themselves heard the words of Christ, or who lived at the same age and the same land. The books of which it is composed were all issued soon after the events took place to which they refer, and were received by other writers of the period immediately succeeding their publication as of divine authority. They were placed in a class by themselves, apart from all other writings: and a deference was paid to them that was conceded to no other record. We have evidence that they have come down to us in their original form, as to all essential particulars.

The confusion of tongues was an evil brought upon man in consequence of his pride of heart and enmity against God; but from it we receive a strong confirmation of the faithful transmission of the Scriptures, as the various languages into which they have been translated are, from their substantial agreement with each other, so many independent testimonies to the purity of their preservation. A similar attestation is derived from another evil, the division of the church into different sections; as all the rest may be regarded as ready to rise in their defence, were any one section to attempt to interpolate or emasculate them. There are also ancient Manuscripts, marked by the clerical errors we may expect to find in works of human manipulation; but all uttering one voice as to the essential verities of the Gospel. It has been the fashion in recent times, to undervalue this kind of testimony to the integrity of the sacred writings; but the church will lay itself open to severe censure, if it allows this outpost in defence of the faith to be withdrawn.

II. THE TRIPITAKA.

The nations of the east that profess the religion of Sákya Muni, regard the three Pitakas* with the deepest reverence, as containing a divine code, in which is all that man can now know of his duty and destiny. They are written in Páli, which, twenty centuries ago, was the vernacular of Mágadha, the province of India in which the Muni lived. It was the dialect used by him in all his public ministrations. The Pitakas are called collectively the Bana, or Word (Sanskrit Vana); and are divided into three principal sections, that are popularly said to refer respectively—1. to the instructions given to the priests; 2. to the laity; and 3. to the gods by whom we are to understand the dwellers in the twenty-six heavens; but these statements are not strictly correct. "The Tripitaka," says Gogerly, "are the Winaya, or Discipline; the Sûtra, or Discourses; and the Abhidharma, or Pre-eminent Doctrines. The last specifies terms with the doctrines connected with them, with explanations and definitions."† The Text and Commentaries extend to nearly ten times the length of the Old and New Testaments.

---

* The great compilation of the Tibetan sacred books, styled the Ká-gyur, in one hundred volumes, is "one and the same compilation" as the Pitakas, "whatever slight discrepancies may be found to exist between the two in minor points." Turnour's Páli Buddhistical Annals, Journ. Bengal As. Soc. July 1837.

† D. J. Gogerly; Journ. Ceylon Branch R. A. S. for 1845, p. 8.

The Scriptures claim to have been "divinely inspired, in-breathed of God." The form in which they appear is modified by the character and circumstances of the writers of the several books. Thus the book of Job bears every sign of having been written in a primitive age: that of Isaiah tells of refinement and luxury, as we listen to the tinkling of the jewelled feet of its mincing maidens, and the bravery of their "tires," "mufflers," and "wimples" gleams before our eyes. The sheikh of Uz only tells us of the Redeemer, that "he shall stand at the latter day upon the earth;" but the more favoured prophet of a nearer age reveals to us that "His name shall be called Wonderful, Counsellor, The mighty God, The everlasting Father, The Prince of Peace," and that "of the increase of his government and peace there shall be no end." So also, the style of David, the royal Psalmist, differs characteristically from that of Amos, the herdman of Tekoah. In the one we have bold, coarse, vehement reproof of the noble and the monarch, as the prophet pleads for the poor, and exposes the robberies connived at by the court. The whispering breath, however, in source and spirit is essentially one, though emitted through instruments of different tone and power.

It is necessary that we repeat these well-known truths—well-known even to the sciolist in biblical lore—in order that the contrast between the two systems we are considering may be seen the more certainly and clearly. We desire to see the Scriptures placed upon what we regard as their rightful throne, when they shall have a name above that of every other book, and before which every mind shall bow, all men listening to the utterances therefrom, as to the oracles of God. We do not contend for all that many sincere men attach to the meaning of the phrase "verbal inspiration"; but we shrink from the thought that what we receive as the word of the ever-blessed Lord of all has in it any element of untruth.

We infer that there is sometimes immediate revelation: and then all we read is as directly from God as the ten words spoken by the divine voice amidst the fires and fears of Sinai. When things are written that were previously known, the inspiration may consist in guidance as to the matter or topic to be recorded; and in the preparation of the record itself, there may have been simply a never-ceasing supervision of the Holy Spirit, preventing the admission of error or mistake; so that, according to the canon for which we now contend, every sentiment and statement in Holy Writ must have been either suggested or verified by God. Of this we have corroborative proof in the the freedom from mistake as to all events in history and all physical phenomena; in which they are in grand contrast to all other archaic writings. As to science, there is no positive statement in them that is contrary to fact. The sun may be spoken of as rising, just as it is spoken of by everybody, men of science included, in our own day; but it is never laid down as an axiom, or insisted on as a truth to be received, that the solar orb actually passes through the circle of travel that is apparent to the senses. In illustration, many things are used in their generally accepted sense: but there is no authoritative teaching of scientific error; and no fact in geology or astronomy, or any other kindred science, universally accepted as true by the best informed men, can be proved to be contrary to any part of the word, when rightly understood and correctly interpreted, that is received by the Church as inspired. When we say that the Bible is the word of God, we mean that it is an immediate emanation from the supreme and eternal Creator and Ruler of the universe; and that, as such every promise it contains may be relied upon with all confidence, every one of its commands is to be obeyed in all its strictness, upon pain of the divine displeasure; and every offer of heavenly aid it presents, in the support of the spirit under trial, or in its efforts to put away sin, may be asked of God, in prayer, with the certainty that it will be granted to the utmost extent in which it can possibly be required.

The Bible professes to contain all that it is necessary for man to know, for his present guidance and future safety. It proclaims unhesitatingly that when read in a reverent spirit, its study will ever be accompanied by a grace divine; cheering, enlightening, and making clean the soul. By this process, all men may test its claim to be a divine record. There may be partial truth in other systems. In them it is presented fitfully, imperfectly, and without authority. But "the law of the Lord is perfect, converting the soul." In the words of man's utterance, we have the cold, lack-lustre, flawed pebble, made to appear radiant by the foil spread beneath it, but the word of God possesses an inherent lustre, "brighter than the noon-day sun." "It cannot be valued with the gold of Ophir, with the precious onyx, or the sapphire. No mention shall be made of coral or of pearls; for its price is above rubies."

The Pitakas too, claim homage from all men, and implicit credence. They say that when there rested upon Sákya Muni, after his struggle with Mára and antagonist demons, the energies and endowments of a supreme Buddha, the whole ocean of truth was clearly presented before him. He could understand perfectly any matter towards which he willed that his attention should be directed, by a process of ratiocination extremely subtle, but in a moment of time as rapid as thought; and he could exhibit, by the mere effort, any exercise of power, creative, transformative, or destructive, in which he willed that there should be the forthputting of his might An order of his disciples, called arhats, was possessed, in a modified degree of the same kind of potency. They were not inspired, *ab extra* but they were intuitively and unerringly intelligent as to all matters connected with religion. They had the kind of infallibility claimed for the pope of Rome, of whom it is said that "he is infallible, not in his personal, but only in his official capacity when dealing with matters connected with the doctrines and discipline of the Church." The system known as Buddhism was for some time preserved in the memories of the arhats, after the death of its founder. It professes to have been enunciated in the exact form in which it is now seen in the Pitakas, immediately after his decease, when the whole of the sacred code was recited in a convocation of arhats, who declared even the number of syllables of which each division was to consist. There were two other similar recitations, by men equally endowed; the second, one hundred years after the first, and the third, one hundred and thirty-four years after the second. In each of these convocations the recitation was perfect and complete, so that no sentence, or part of a sentence, was omitted.

Upon the truth of these statements much must depend; for if their correctness could be proved, it would confer upon the Pitakas an authenticity that they now lack; but, according to the testimony of their own adherents, 450 years elapsed after their first rehearsal, and 350 after the second before they were committed to writing. The northern Buddhists say that the event took place B. C. 153. But in either case, they are thus deprived of an authority as a record of facts, and can only be received as a repertory of ancient myths, legends, and traditions, such as are treasured up in the memory, and heard from the lips of the aged of nearly all nations; or as the exponents of a system attributed to certain teachers and philosophers, who are men of bold and lofty thought, but mistaken in many of their conclusions; and in their claim to the possession of supremacy in the realm of truth, to be regarded as pretenders, or as wishing to assume an authority to which they have no patent of right. In these respects there is an important difference between the Bible, which may be called a contemporaneous record, and the Dharma, which can have no pretension to be regarded as an authority upon the same ground.

III. TRADITIONS.

All who are called Christians do not regard the Scriptures of the Old and New Testaments as "the sole rule of faith." "The Catholic rule of faith," we are told by Dr. Milner, "is not merely the written word of God, but the whole word of God, written or unwritten, in other words, Scripture and tradition, and these propounded and explained by the Christian church." With this must agree, as to the value of tradition, the other ancient churches of Christendom; as they all teach doctrines, and practice ceremonies, that have no warrant from the canonical Bible.

There is this difference between the followers of Christ and the professors of Buddhism, that among the former there are some who reject tradition entirely, except as confirmatory or explanatory of the written word, and there are others who assert the authority of both Scripture and tradition, regarding them substantially as having an equal claim to their respect and obedience; but the whole of the Buddhist faith is founded on tradition exclusively, inasmuch as the whole written word was, with them, at its commencement, a collection of traditions; and these not of recent origin, so that their truth might be tested by the memory of men still living. The place at which they were committed permanently to the palm-leaf was also as far from the locality of Sákya Muni's reputed residence as the metropolis of Britain from the usual dwelling-place of the apostles.

The whole of the Pitakas, including the Text and the Commentary* were taken to the island of Ceylon in the memory of the priest Mahinda, son of the supreme ruler of India, B. C. 307.† By him the Commentaries were translated into Singhalese. The venerated word was orally transmitted, by successive generations of the monks, until about the year B. C. 90, when, "in order that the religion might endure for ages, the monks recorded the same in books." The necessity of having some authoritative standard of faith was caused by the number of heresies that had begun to appear on every hand; and that bade fair to destroy the integrity of the system entirely, by throwing the disciples of the Dharma into inextricable confusion.

* The Commentaries are confessedly much more modern than the Text. Gogerly; Journ. Ceylon Branch R. A. S. for 1845, p. 8. When additions are made to the original Text, the priests affirm that those portions are of equal authority with the rest, as they were equally recited in the three Convocations. Ib. p. 92.

† Or B. C. 246

The authoritative transcription is said to have taken place in the cave temple of Alu, in Ceylon, during the reign of Wattagamini, who flourished between B. C. 101 and 76. In the anarchy of succeeding periods, the original Commentaries were lost; but as they were still preserved in Singhalese, about the year A. D. 430, they were re-translated from Singhalese into Páli by the brahman Buddhaghôsa, who was sent to Ceylon for the purpose from the continent of India.* The name of the translation, which signifies "the voice of Buddha," or "the voice of the wise," suggests the thought that it may be unreal; and it is probable that it was not by one man that this work was performed, and that it was not completed in one age. Subsequently, the whole of the canon was lost by the Singhalese, and the recension of the Tripitaka now in use is received from Burma or Siam. Whatever value they may have as the most perfect compendium we possess of an ancient faith, their origin is involved in too much obscurity to allow of their being unhesitatingly relied upon, even by those who are most earnest and sincere in their attachment to Buddhism as a guide to "the city of peace."

The historical and scientific errors with which they abound have been recorded and exposed in a monograph written with this design.† We shall presently have to refer to their exaggerations in chronology, which have no parallel, even in the most unrestrained flights of eastern fancy. As to science, it may be enough to say, that they gravely speak of a mountain in the centre of the earth, Maha Meru, more than a million miles high; of a sea, eight hundred thousand miles deep; and of fishes more than ten thousand miles in length.

---

* The Commentaries of Buddhaghôsa are very voluminous, and furnish both a Commentary and a glossary for the whole of the Pitakas. Turnour; Journ. Bengal A. S. July, 1837.

† "Legends and Theories of the Buddhists; by R. Spence Hardy." London: Williams and Norgate. 1866.

CHAPTER II.

THE EXISTENCE OF GOD.

I. THEISM OF THE SCRIPTURES. II. ATHEISM OF THE PITAKAS.

I. THEISM OF THE SCRIPTURES.

The most ancient writer whose works have come down to our own time enters into no argument to prove that there is a God, nor does he represent God as preparing man for the birth of revelation by any solemn announcement of this primary truth. Unlike other cosmogonies the biblical record takes it for granted as a fact requiring no demonstration. The voice of God, and the glory of the divine presence, were in themselves proof of His existence, majesty, and power. "That God is, and that He is a rewarder of them that diligently seek Him," must have been made known to man at the earliest dawn of his being from the circumstances in which he was placed; as we cannot suppose that God would fling him into existence without teaching him all that it was absolutely necessary for him to know. The knowledge thus conveyed at first by immediate revelation would afterwards be communicated by man to his fellow man. It is long before we have any intimation that the existence of God was either denied or forgotten. The thought would linger long in the minds of men, and there would be glimpses of the fact when a clear knowledge of its reality was beginning to fade away amidst the deepening darkness and uncertainty of tradition. It seems never to have been regained by the exercise of unassisted reason, when once lost; nor have all the thinkings of the sage ever added one single attribute to those which are ascribed to God in the Scriptures: whence we may infer, that we are indebted to revelation for our present knowledge of the very existence of God. But though man cannot "by searching find out God," he has in his own heart, in the rule of the world, in the earth upon which he treads, and in the radiant heavens that gleam above him, confirmative proof that there is one Lord, one God, "high over all."

II. ATHEISM OF THE PITAKAS.

The contrast between the Hebrew and the Aryan teachers is here decided and essential. In the Pitakas the existence is denied of one God; of a Being who is supreme, infinite in all the attributes of His divinity, and subsisting from eternity to eternity. In proof of this statement, we may refer to the Brahma Játa, which is the first sermon in the series of Discourses attributed to Sákya Muni, a translation of which, from the pen of the Rev. D. J Gogerly, appears in the second number of the Journal of the Ceylon Branch of the Royal Asiatic Society, published in 1847. But in order to understand more clearly the extract we are about to make, we must premise that there are periodical destructions and re-productions of the mundane system; and that in this system there are various heavens, divided into two classes, the inferior (déwa-lôka) and the superior (brahma-lôka). When a section of the heavens has ceased to exist, and another is produced, the new worlds are at first uninhabited.

"At that time a being, in consequence either of the period of residence in Abassara (the sixth of the superior heavens) being expired, or in consequence of some deficiency of merit preventing him from living there the full period, ceased to exist in Abassara, and is re-produced in the uninhabited Brahma Wimáno. He there a spiritual being, having intellectual pleasures, is self-resplendent, traverses the atmosphere, and is for a long time in the enjoyment of happiness. After living there a very long time alone, being indisposed to continue in solitude, his desires are excited, and he says, Would that another being were dwelling in this place. At that immediate juncture another being, either on account of a deficiency of merit or on account of the period of residence being expired, ceasing to exist in Abassara springs into life in the Brahma Wimáno, in the vicinity of the first one. They are both of them spiritual beings, have intellectual pleasures, are self-resplendent, traverse the atmosphere, and are for a long time in the enjoyment of happiness. Then the following thoughts arose in him who was the first existent in that world: I am Brahma, Maha Brahma, the Supreme, the Invincible, the Omnicient, the Ruler, the Lord of all, the Maker, the Creator. I am the Chief, the Disposer of all, the Controller of all, the Universal Father of all. This being was made by me. How does this appear? Formerly I thus thought: Would that another being were in this place. Upon my volition this being came here. Those beings also who first obtained an existence there, thought: This illustrious Brahma is Maha Brahma, the Supreme, the Invincible, the Omnicient, the Ruler, the Lord, the Maker, the Creator of all. He is the chief, the Disposer of all things, the Controller of all, the Universal Father. We were created by him; for we see that he was first here, and that we have since then obtained existence. Furthermore, he who was the first that obtained existence there, has a very long period of existence, exceeds in beauty and is possessed of immense power: but those who follow him are short lived, of inferior beauty, and of little power. It then happens, that one of these beings ceasing to exist there, is born in this world, and afterwards retires from society and becomes a recluse. Being thus a houseless priest, he subjects his passions, is constant and persevering in the practice of virtue, and by profound and correct meditation attains that mental tranquility by which he recollects his immediately previous state of existence, but none before that. He therefore says: That illustrious Brahma is Maha Brahma, the Supreme, the Invincible, the Omnicient, the Ruler, the Lord, the Maker, the Creator. He is the Chief, the Disposer of all things, the Controller of all, the Universal Father. That Brahma, by whom we were created, is ever-during, immutable, the eternal, the unchangeable, continuing the same for ever. But we, who have been created by this illustrious Brahma, are not ever-during; we are mutable, short-lived, mortal, and were born here. This is the first reason on account of which some Samanas and Brahmins hold the eternal existence of some things, but not of others, and teach concerning the soul and the world, that some things are eternal, and that other things are not eternal."

It was evidently known to Sákya Muni, that there were reasoners in the world who acknowledged the existence of a Supreme Being, "the Creator of all things, the Controller of all things, the Eternal, and the Unchangeable," but this conclusion is said to proceed from "an incorrect understanding." It arises from the want of a proper insight into the causes of events, and is propounded by a being who belongs to an inferior order, and is possessed of only imperfect merit.

The atheism of the Dharma has been denied; but upon insufficient authority. In support of this opinion, the stanzas have been quoted that were spoken by Sákya Muni at the time he became a supreme Buddha,

"Through various transmigrations
I must travel, if I do not discover
The Builder whom I seek:

Painful are repeated transmigrations,
I have seen the Architect (and said)
Thou shalt not build me another house;
Thy rafters are broken,
Thy roof-timbers scattered;
My mind is detached (from all existing objects)
I have attained to the extinction of desire."

By the architect here spoken of we are not to understand a personal entity: but the non-intelligent cause of the repetition of existence.

Upon this vital principle of the system, affecting so many subordinate branches, the deliverance of the late Professor Wilson is unhesitating and conclusive. "Belief in a Supreme Being, the Creator and Ruler of the universe," he says, "is unquestionably a modern graft upon the unqualified atheism of Sákya Muni; it is still of very limited recognition. In none of the standard authorities translated by M. Burnouf or Mr. Gogerly is there the slightest allusion to a First-Cause, the existence of whom is incompatible with the fundamental Buddhist dogma of the eternity of all existence. The doctrine of an Adi Buddha, a first Buddha, in the character of a Supreme Creator, which has found its way into Nepaul, and perhaps into Western Tibet, is entirely local, as is that of the Dyáni Buddhas, and the Bodhisatwas, their sons and agents in creation, as described by Mr. Hodgson."

The sect in Nepaul to which the Professor refers is that of the Aishwarikas. They admit of the existence of an immaterial essence, who is said to be "supreme, infinite, self-existent, before all, without beginning, infini-formed and formless, the cause of all things, separate from all things, the cause of the well-being of all existence in the three worlds."

In the histories of Sákya Muni, six heretics are frequently named, and their principal tenets are detailed. According to Brigandet, the last of the six teachers "boldly asserted the existence of a Supreme Being, Creator of all that exists, and alone worthy of receiving adoration": but his teachings are pronounced by the orthodox to be false and dangerous.

As all beings, without exception, unless they have entered one of the "paths" that lead to nirvána, extinction, are subject alike to the law of transmigratory mutation, an eternal Creator cannot possibly exist in any world.

The founders of both the schools, Northern and Southern, were evidently acquainted with the theistic doctrine: but by the latter it was entirely rejected, and among the former regarded as the tenet of a sect—but to what extent the belief prevailed does not appear. The incompatibility of theism with the teachings of the Dharma will be more clearly seen when their speculations on the origin of the world, as presented in the next chapter, have passed under review.

CHAPTER III.

THE ORIGIN OF THE UNIVERSE.

I. CREATION. II. CAUSATION. III. KARMA. IV. SENTIENT EXISTENCE. V. FORMER HISTORY. VI. THE DELUGE. VII. LONGEVITY.

I. CREATION.

In the Scriptures we read, that "in the beginning God created the heaven and the earth." St. John tells us, that all things were made by the Word, who was "with God," and "was God," and "without Him was not anything made that was made." We learn from the apostle Paul, that "by Him (who is 'the image of the invisible God') were all things created, that are in heaven and that are in earth, visible and invisible, whether they be thrones, or dominions, or principalities, or powers, all things were created by Him and for Him. And He is before all things, and by Him all things consist." These terms are all-inclusive. In a few words, we have all matter and all spirit; the whole kosmos, the universe. There may be some controversy relative to the meaning of the word *bara*, as to whether it refers to "creation out of nothing," or merely to "arrangement" or "formation;" but the sense in which it is here used may be inferred from other portions of the Scriptures of truth. "Through faith we understand that the worlds were framed by the word of God, so that things which are seen were not made of things which do appear." We thus learn, that the visible creation was not made of matter previously existing; it was not a reducing to order, or a vivifying, of particles or atoms that were in existence before the operation upon these of the power of God. With this agrees the Hebrew notion of a post-prophetic age. "God did not create them (heaven and earth) out of things already existant." Macc. vii. 28, We conclude, therefore, that the world in which we live has not, in any sense, had an existence coeval with the existence of God, as was almost universally taught in the old philosophies. It is not a fragment of the divine subsistence or essence; nor is that essence the basis or substratum of the objective universe. It is not a mere emanation, or outflowing; but a created thing, with a beginning, essentially distinct and separate from the nature of Him who bade it be, the eternal and subsisting "I am that I am."

II. CAUSATION.

From the instructions given by Sákya Muni to his disciples we learn, that there are certain subjects they are to regard as being beyond the reach of their comprehension: and as all research in relation to them would be purposeless and without profit, they are admonished not to attempt the investigation. In this category he includes all speculation as to the origin of the world. It is not so prominent a doctrine with him as with the Brahmans (though held by him, under another form) that all that is perceived by the senses is an illusion. His doubts in relation to existence are not propounded so much concerning things visible, as about the ego, or the self. If he denies that there is any reality in the idea of sentient existence, it is rather to dissuade men from the exercises that produce ego-ism—including in this thought as a primary principle all that induces them to seek sensuous gratification—than to assert the non-existence of an outer world. We may anticipate, therefore, that Buddhist authors will be more sparing than other eastern writers in the attention they pay to creation or to kosmo-plastic speculation.

We shall be the better able to understand their notions on the origin of the various beings and things around us, when we have learnt their ideas about the formative and preservative processes that are continually exerting their influence, in all ages and in all worlds. There were always worlds, in most respects homogeneous with those now in existence.

That "all things proceed from some cause," is an oft-repeated axiom of Sákya Muni.* It is found in the discourses attributed to him, and upon ancient slabs now in existence, and in formularies still repeated by the devout. All sentient beings are produced by the karma (action, regarded ethically, as good or bad) of previous births. Fire, and all vegetable productions arise from causes of the same identical nature as themselves;

* Among the philosophers who "reason from the past," there is a class who hold that the world and themselves are uncaused. With these Buddha "acknowledges that there is no creative cause of existence, but denies that existence is uncaused, attributing causation to moral congruity." Gogerly; Ceylon Friend, Sept, 1838.

as fire comes from fire, and seed from seed. The earth, its mountains, the elements (except fire) and the visible worlds, are produced by the seasons; by which appears to be meant, periodic intervals, referring to the monsoons of the tropics and the successive revolutions of the celestial bodies. These producing energies are not instrumentalities in the hand of an intelligent agent, but are themselves primary causes, acting without any influence extraneous to themselves.

In the Rájawalia, a Singhalese historical work, it is said that after the destruction of the world that existed previous to the one in which we now live, "by the entire karma of all sentient existences," a rain began to fall; but how it was formed, or whence it came, we are not told. "By the same power," a wind arose, by which the waters were evaporated: and after their desiccation, the dry land appeared; which, in process of time, became inhabited by a race or beings who came into existence by the apparitional birth. They had at first an inherent splendour that illuminated the whole world; and when this was lost, they assembled together, and "by this united Karma," caused the sun to appear, and then the moon and the planets; the sun on the first day of the week, the moon on the second day, and so on. Thus, the karma of previously-existing beings was the cause by which the world came into existence.*

In a conversation recorded as having taken place between Nágaséna, a priest, and Milinda, king of Sagal, a little before the time of Christ, it is stated by the sage, and acknowledged by his co-religionists, that production is always from something that previously existed. Before the house was produced, there was the stone in the quarry and the wood in the forest; before the tree, the fruit; before the potter's vessel, the moist clay; before the music-strain, the instrument; and before the fire, the burning-glass, the sunray, and the shred of dry cloth. *Ex nihilo nihil fit.* This may appear to be contradicted by what is called the apparitional birth, in which sentient beings start up into existence, in a moment from nothingness and vacancy; but even under these circumstances there is always some one in existence previous to the appearance of the new existence, by whom the new existence is caused.

* The conclusion has been controverted by a Páli scholar of the highest authority; but he does not give any reason for its denial. Gogerly's Lecture on Buddhism, 1861. In another work he has said previously, "It is by Karma that the worlds are framed and modified." Ceylon Friend, Dec. 1837.

In the multiplication of existences through the mystic power called irdhi, the phantoms that are said to be formed arise from the will of the ascetic; but though they appear to act as sentient existences, the more thoughtful Buddhists would probably say that they have no reality, and are mere illusions.

III. KARMA.

As karma is the key-thought of nearly all Buddhistic speculation, we must seek to understand, as correctly as we can, the meaning of the term. It is literally, "that which is done." It is represented as having three constituents: merit, demerit, and neutrality, that which is neither good nor bad. When Sákya Muni was asked what was the nature of karma, he replied, "All sentient beings have their own individual karma. It comes by inheritance (not by parentage, but from previous births): it is the cause of all good or evil; it is the (ethical) difference of karma that causes the difference in the lot of man, so that some are mean and others exalted, some are miserable and others are happy."* "Karma is like the shadow, that always accompanied the body. But it cannot be said that it is here, or that it is there; in this place or in that place; the locality in which it resides cannot be pointed out. Thus, there is a fruit tree, but at present not bearing; at this time it cannot be said that its fruit is in this part of the tree or in that; nevertheless, the fruit exists in the tree. It is the same with karma."† With these statements, the adherents of the Karmika system among the Nepaulese are in perfect agreement. "The actions of a man's former birth constitute his destiny. Karma accompanies everyone, everywhere, every instant, through the forest, and across the ocean, and over the highest mountains, into heaven and into hell."‡ It is said that there can be no acquirement of (meritorious) karma in an age when there is no Buddha; nor in a region where Buddha is unknown, nor by non-human beings, except from the hearing of the sacred bana; nor by the inhabitants of any of the hells.

In the present state of human knowledge, with the imperfect mental powers we now possess, we must expect that there will be mysteries connected with the universe of being: but among all the numerous efforts that have been made to explain the phenomena of existence, that of the Buddhist is the least logical or conclusive. It possesses an appearance of simplicity:

---

* Manual of Buddhism, p. 446. † Ib. p. 441.
‡ Hodgson's Illustrations.

but it is mere assertion without any attempt to prove its authority, and the manner in which it is said to operate contradicts our reason. No power can act in any place to which its influence does not, in some way or other, extend, and no agency can exert an influence upon any object with which it cannot communicate; yet karma must do this, if it does what it is said to do. The Buddhists seek to evade this conclusion; but it is by an agreement put in their own inconclusive manner. "There is one man," they say, "watching another, who is at the verge of a precipice. He is moved thereby; starts up from his seat through fear; and is greatly agitated. What means of communication was there between the man in safety and the man in danger? Yet the man in danger acts thus powerfully upon the man who is distant from him, and with whom he has no means of communication. So may karma act upon that from which it is distant and isolated."

There must be an essential difference between karma as an aggregate energy; and karma as a personal possession, controlling the circumstances of the individual. But how the karma of a given individual can be an outflow from the karma of a successive series of individuals who have existed before him, from the last of whom he sprang, is an incomprehensible mystery. The difficulty is increased when the karma is regarded as the aggregate of all potency, forming worlds and controlling all existence. We have here an energy that is beyond all conception in the might of its working; and yet is a mere abstraction. It takes the place of what is sometimes called "nature," a term just as difficult to understand. We require clearer information than that which is now within our reach, before we can explain the working of this occult principle; unless from the first it was involved in inextricable confusion by its original promoters.

IV. SENTIENT EXISTENCE.

By the influence of karma the Buddhist attempts to account for the changes that are ever taking place in the world; but respecting the commencement of existence he offers no explanation. "Priests," said Sákya Muni, "the initial point of the series of successive transmigrations is not known." All that we can learn is, that the seed comes from a previous seed, the egg from a previous egg; but how the first seed or the first egg was produced, we cannot discover. No beginning or end can be pointed out in a geometrical circle, and it is the same with the sequence of existence. The circle of being is demonstrated by the Muni in a formula that has a prominent place in all Buddhist works of a speculative character; and is received in all countries where the Dharma is known.

It is heard in Nepaul and Tibet, repeated in China, and taught in nearly the same terms, in Burma and Ceylon.

In this synopsis of the various phases of being, the initiative of existence is represented as being *áwidya*, ignorance. This term means literally, "the unperceived, the unfelt, the unknown, or the unascertainable." But it is only one link in a circle, first named because the enumeration of the several links must begin somewhere. It is not the beginning of existence, as this is hid from the understanding of all but a supreme Buddha. We are left in doubt whether áwidya (non-knowledge) is to be regarded as an active quality or a mere negation; and it may be that nothing more is intended by the expression, than that the manner of the origin of the world cannot be discovered or explained. However strange it may appear to us, that merit and demerit which are regarded as the second link in the chain, can flow from ignorance, the postulate is in entire consonance with Buddhist thought. In the system attributed to Sákya Muni, it is received as a truism, as a thing not to be disputed, that effects may proceed from causes with which they have no homogeniety of relationship, and that cannot possibly produce the consequences that are affirmed. With them the power of the golden harp of Orpheus would be no fable. Organisms and sentient intelligences of every kind may be produced from that which has in itself no concrete being or objective existence. Hence, when we are told that ignorance produces merit or demerit, and then consciousness, and all the other constituents in the combination of sentient existence, it is in vain for us to enquire how this can be; it must suffice to know that such is the dictum of the all-knowing sage; but the error arises from the confounding of two classes of causes, entirely distinct from each other, the moral and the material, and in the attributing to one species the effects that can only be produced by the other species.

V. FORMER HISTORY.

This story of the past is to be learnt, from that of the present. There have been repetitions endless of worlds like our own. As one mango-fruit has been proceded by another, of the like kind, so has one seed been proceded by another seed, and one world by another world of the same character and type. There is little originality in the mental creations of the Buddhists. In their mythology we look in vain for that variety of colour and circumstance that ever accompanies the conceptions of the far-seeing. There is much in it that is weird and strange; but its most cherished sympathies are not human, and there is too often an entire absence of moral in its myths.

We read many of its stories with the same kind of thought with which we should listen to a nursery tale of the higher order, or to the simple incidents of a village ballad. In so extensive a literature there must, of necessity, be some incidents and passages to which this criticism will not apply; but they are rare as the mimic sail of the delicate nautilus upon the far-stretching sea.

The Bible presents no criteria from which we can calculate the age of the world. "In the beginning," is its grand exordium; but *when* the beginning was, it does not tell us. The principal event in the ancient history of man is known as the deluge, when all perished from off the face of the earth, except the members of one family. The date of this occurrence may be stated to have been about 4,000 years previous to the present time. Independently of the Hebrew Scriptures, were any one, guided by the rules of modern research, to set himself to discover, from all the sources at his command, the age in which the race of man began, he would have to pause at this period, from the inability to discover any link that would connect it with a previous era. We may be told of arrows with flint heads, and of other relics of a barbarous age; but we have no nexus by which we can bridge over the distance between the stone-axe period and that of the pyramid. We have no proof that the savage with so rude an instrument slowly and gradually rose into the man of science who built the monumental sepulchres that throw their shadows athwart the sands of the Nilotic valley. This would have required ages for its accomplishment, and of such a process of gradual perfectioning we have no trace.

When the imagination has unlimited range, we may expect to meet with events and circumstances that are without the pale of ordinary occurrence, and that set at nought the sobriety of historical truth. In these circumstances, time and space can be extended to infinity.

Hence, when we pass from the writings of Moses to those of the Buddhist recorder, we are at once confronted by numbers that startle us by their immensity. According to them, the first monarch, Sammata, as well as some 23 of his successors, reigned an asankya each. To understand what an *asankya* is, we must turn away from the numeration table of our schoolboy days, and pass onward until we have before us, according to one authority, a unit followed by 140 cyphers, and according to another, a unit followed by 4,000,000 cyphers or as many as would extend 44,000 feet, in numerals of the ordinary size. The Pitakas give us detailed accounts of events that took place in ages a hundred thousandfold more ancient than the era of this first king; but the greater part of what they tell us, in relation to language, realms, mountains, rivers, manners, customs, forms of government, and systems of religion, is so exactly in unison with the character of the period in which the writers themselves lived, that we can only receive their accounts as highly magnified exaggerations of the present, and not as actual and ancient occurrence. We have also the same products in the animal and vegetable kingdoms. There are monstrosities of fearful size and shape; but these are principally resident in other worlds.

In another department of historical notification there is a partial agreement between the Pitakas and the Scriptures. They commence with man in the perfection of his being and present to us no rude or embryonic era. The first men were possessed of supernatural endowments; and though they lost their original purity and power, they never degenerated into savageism. But the Buddhist writers, in other statements are less in consistence with known fact: as they start with a series of kings, resident at Rajagaha or some other historical city of India who reigned in the utmost magnificence, and were possessed of magic power, so that they could summon into their treasury myriads of gems by the mere clapping of the hand. The earlier Vedas are here more trustworthy; as the ancestors and contemporaries of the rishis are represented as being nomads, hunters, cattle tenders, and fierce warriors, whose stirring songs told of a migration from a colder country beyond the snowy mountains.

VI. THE DELUGE.

The Noachic flood has its counterpart upon the page of the Dharma; according to the teachings of which, the mundane system is destroyed, in its periodical changes, seven times by fire, the eighth time by water, and the sixty-fourth by wind.

The last destruction was by fire; after which rain began to fall, first as drift, or in drops small as the dew, and last of all in masses that were miles in size, until the space to which many worlds extend was entirely inundated. A mighty wind then arose, which agitated the surging waters of the deep, until they were all evaporated, except those which form the ocean and its tributaries, and fill the cavity under the earth. The next destruction will be by fire; previous to which a celestial being will appear in the world with streaming eyes and a form of woe, proclaiming the nature of the coming danger, thereby warning mankind, and exhorting them to avoid all evil, and exercise kindness towards each other.

The deluge was an event of too terrific a character not to be long remembered in the traditions of the earlier nations; and accordingly we find reference to it in most of the ancient legends that are still extant. There is not one of them in which there is not agreement, in some detail or other, with the Mosaic record. The coincidences are too numerous and definite not to have had a common origin. With the Hebrew historian the flood is a part of one grand chain of historical sequence, and its omission would leave other incidents, of primary importance in the working out of the divine economy, without an explanation. It is the chain that separates the rifts that appear on both sides of the era in which it took place. The events in other diluvian narratives may arise naturally from the scenes presented by Moses, as many of them tend to confirm and elucidate his statements. But there is no single tradition or legend that can be taken in the same way, and regarded as the basis of the rest. The older record is the source whence the others radiate or whence they originate; in tradition, they become the more unhistorical the further they proceed from the era of Noah.

VII. LONGEVITY.

In the period to which the lives of the antediluvians were prolonged, we have another fact of a character so remarkable, that we may expect to meet with references to it in the archaic memorials that have survived to the present time. But here, again, the Buddhists have distorted possible occurrence into palpable extravagance. According to their teachings, the first men lived to a period that can only be equalled among ourselves by some astronomical cycle or geological era, with its unfathomable milleniums. The biblical account may have been recorded to prove to us, that if man in his present circumstances, exposed to accident and disease, as contradistinguished from the time of his innocence, could live to the age of a thousand years, it was possible for him to have been longer preserved from death, by a further extension of the sanative and preservative power with which he was gifted, until, without seeing death, he was accounted worthy of being translated, like Enoch, to the higher home of God.

Thus, in the waters that we are told preceded the present mundane economy, their gradual increase and the means by which they were assuaged; in the longevity of the first race of men, and its subsequent diminution: in the warning voice heard previous to the world's destruction, and in the mode by which its ruin will be next effected, we have an echo, faint and broken, of truths presented in the word of God. As it comes to us from afar, we listen to it with interest, from its illustrations of revealed occurrence: but its words are too indefinite, and its sentences too unconnected, to allow of our receiving them as anything further than semblances of fact.

CHAPTER IV.

THE ORIGIN OF EVIL.

I. THE FALL. II. INDIAN TRADITIONS. III. THE COMING OF EVIL. IV. LIKENESS TO SCRIPTURE.

I. THE FALL.

An answer to the question, Whence did evil proceed? has been attempted by nearly all the sages among whom the existence of evil is acknowledged. Its difficulties do not affect the historical character of revelation. Evil existed before the appearance of man on the earth. "There were fallen angels before there were fallen men." In the first man it was a communicated taint, and not an original or inherent corruption though now universally prevalent. How it originated, we are not told by God; and as man cannot penetrate into the mysteries of other worlds, and is unable to explain numberless phenomena in his own, we must be contented to remain without a solution of the problem, unless further light is thrown upon it from some supernatural source.

When the veil is uplifted that reveals to us the primeval position of man, he appears before us as living in innocence; the resident in a garden in Eden, and its possessor, in which all around him is "beauty to his eye or music to his ear." Like all other created intelligences, he has given to him certain duties that he is required to perform. For perseverance in righteousness his reward will be great; for the commission of sin his punishment will be fearful. The duties imposed upon him are of a two-fold character. There is something that he is to do, and something that he is not to do. He is to dress and keep the beautiful garden in which he walked as the vicegerent of the Most High, eating of all its produce, except of the fruit of one tree, which he is forbidden to touch, upon pain of the forfeiture of all the privileges of his existence. The happiness of this first man, Adam, and of the second self whom God gave him, Eve, excited the envy of the fallen angels;

and their prince, Satan, tempted these privileged beings to transgress the divine command, under the specious insinuation that they would thereby become "as God," in a higher degree, with the power to understand branches of knowledge now unknown. Fast by the forbidden tree was another tree, "the tree of life," the eating of which may have been intended as a sacramental act, as "the outward and visible sign of an inward and spiritual grace." It appears to have been appointed by God to be an assurance to man that the power he needed to continue in the path of righteousness would be forthcoming so long as he sought it in a right spirit, and to be an act of humble confession, on the part of man, of his dependence upon God for every privilege he possessed. It may have been in the neglect of this means of grace that his first deviation from the path of duty commenced, which robbed him of his strength, and prepared him for the successful onslaught of his enemies; as with the Titan of Israel in the house of Delilah. But be this thought fanciful, or be it not; man listened to the subtle tempter rather than o God; the place of peril was approached; a fruit was broken tfrom the prohibited tree; it was eaten; then came death and all our woe.

II. INDIAN TRADITIONS.

There is some agreement between the traditions of India and these statements of holy writ. In our day there are many men of note who seek to trace the origin of their species to something as far as possible from humanity, and seem to rejoice in the paternity of the ape or the gorilla. But the fables that were framed in former ages looked in an entirely opposite direction. Many of them represent the first men as wise and pure, or as fragments of the divine essence, either separated therefrom, as the water-drop from the fulness of the ocean, or as appearing in a form illusory, like the reflections of the sun in the multitudinous waves of the agitated lake. The beings who were created by Brahmá were at first endowed with righteousness and perfect faith; their hearts were without guile; they were made free from soil by the observance of sacred institutes.*

III. THE COMING OF EVIL.

We are informed by the Bana, that after the waters caused by the rain that fell upon the earth at the commencement of he present cycle (kalpa) had evaporated or subsided, there was

---

* Wilson's Vishnu Purána.

everywhere darkness. In process of time, when the merit of the beings inhabiting the superior heavens had become exhausted, or had lost its conservative power, and could no longer secure them in that high estate, they became residents in the world now inhabited by men. They received their existence by the apparitional birth. In a moment they came into being, like the spark struck from the smitten flint, or the lightning-gleam flashed across the sky in the hour of storm. There was then no sun ; nor was there need of one; as their bodies were self-luminous, the light from them extending everywhere, and they could rise into the air, or pass from one place to another, with the swiftness of thought. The night was as the day in its brightness; all seasons were alike propitious; and happiness reigned on every hand, in unbroken succession. They were free from all appetite or passion; they required no food, and the distinction of sex was unknown. Thus they lived for ages in the undisturbed enjoyment of existence. But there gradually formed upon the surface of the earth a substance like the scum seen upon milk that has been boiled. It was mucilaginous; but pure as "the virgin honey in the cell of the bee." By this time the luminousness of their primitive state had lost its former brightness, and they became gross and partially organized. A desire for food arose; and one of the beings having applied a portion of the honey-like substance to his mouth, its taste was so pleasant, that it excited the wish for more; and the stirrings of appetite, hunger and thirst, were now felt. This was followed by other deteriorations They had no longer an inherent lustre. As some partook more eagerly than others of the grateful aliment, that had now become a necessity, their skin became coarse in proportion, and their colour dark. As time passed on, and the grossness of the beings increased, the original substance disappeared from the earth; but in its stead a pure kind of rice was produced, by partaking of which the inferior apertures of the body were formed, the generative powers were developed, and passion and its indulgence quickly followed. The more temperate preserved their lustre for a longer period; but by degrees enmity and every kind of evil came into existence, like things loathsome and monstrous from the compost of the fermenting cesspool.*

IV. LIKENESS TO SCRIPTURE.

By these old legends the Buddhists are taught that before the appearance of sentient existence, "darkness covered

* Journ. Bengal As. Soc. 1833, p. 385.

the face of the deep," and, that mankind were originally homogeneous, though not descended from one single parent. All men were "unsoiled," free from passion and unrest. Of the image of God the Dharma knows nothing, but the liniaments it gives to man primeval are divine. It was from partaking of food that he lost his virgin purity and radiance. In many of these traditions there is a scantling of truth; a verisimilitude that contrasts favourably with the myths of other systems. It is worthy of remark that the first dispute that arose in the world was from a difference in colour; and that for a long period there was an acknowledged separation of the pure from the impure; after which the lawlessness of the depraved led to the formation of secular government, and the appointment of an order of men who were to restrain the wayward and instruct the unwise. The legends, however, lack moral weight. We rise from their perusal with no hatred to sin, and with no thought that a power not our own is needed to replace us in our original state of high and holy privilege. There is no reference as in most traditions of the far past to the service of the priest, or to any one who offers sacrifice or presents an atonement. As no hand of help is needed, none is provided, and none sought; but there is given to man no song of triumph as in Christianity, uplifting him far above all that is sad and sinful, and enabling him to cry out even in the agony of the mortal struggle, "Thanks be unto God, which giveth us the victory through our Lord Jesus Christ." From the teachings of the Bible alone, the source of this confidence can be learnt: and from the influence of the Holy Spirit alone can its possession be secured.

BOOK II.

THE PERSON.

CHAPTER I.

PRE-EXISTENCE.

I. THE THEME. II. THE DIFFICULTY. III. OF CHRIST. IV. OF FORMER BUDDHAS. V. THE PROMISE. VI. THE PERIOD. VI. THE WISH.

I. THEME.

We approach the adytum of the great theme we have proposed as the principal subject of our research and elucidation with unsandalled feet and lowly reverence, as utterly unworthy to pass its threshold, or tread the crystal pavement upon which the reflection of the shekina has fallen as with "the brightness of the Father's glory." But we would humbly hope that He who spake of Himself as "greater than Solomon," and "greater than Jonah," and of the Father Himself as "greater than all," and whose inspired apostle said that "the High Priest of our profession" was "counted worthy of more glory than Moses," will not regard it as an act of irreverence if we attempt to set forth the glory of the Lord's Christ, as compared with the character given to the reputed Buddha, whom myriads ignorantly worship.

II. THE DIFFICULTY.

The difficulty connected with the working out of the contrast we propose to make, becomes the more apparent, when it is remembered that the Sákya Muni of modern Buddhism is a creature of the imagination alone, though formed, it may be, from the glimmerings of true tradition: so that the comparison is really between history and legend; the facts of truth and the fictions of fancy; between the "Word of Life," of whom the apostle John could say, "which we have heard, which we have seen with our eyes, which we have looked upon and our hands have handled," and a phantom formed from the brain of ascetics musing under the palm-tree of the orient, who note down dreams and attaching to them names, call their records history. In all the acts we ascribe to Buddha, we must be understood as speaking of what is said, rather than of that which was ever done; it is the attributed we have to deal with and not the actual or proven.

III. OF CHRIST.

The first subject that claims attention in this department of our investigation is connected with the dogma of pre-existence. "In the beginning was the Word," "and the Word was made flesh." John i. 1, 14. Jesus said to the Jews—who asked of him a sign that he had come from God, like that of the manna which their fathers did eat in the desert—that he was himself the bread of God, "which cometh down from heaven and giveth life unto the world." And when they were startled by so bold a declaration, he repeated it and said, "I came down from heaven not to do Mine own will but the will of Him that sent Me." He had previously announced to Nicodemus, as the shadows of night hid from public exposure the shrinking Pharisee, that "no man hath ascended up to heaven, but He that came down from heaven, even the Son of Man which is in heaven." John iii. 13. That he was not a celestial being, formed for some great purpose, and after his creation sent forth from the midst of "the excellent glory," that he might perform the behest of God, was clear, as he declared to the listeners in the temple, "Before Abraham was, I am;" and when the hour of his glorification drew nigh, in prayer presented before the eternal throne he said, "O, Father, glorify Me with thine own self, with the glory which I had with Thee before the world was." John xvii. 5. We hereby learn that Jesus Christ is "the Lord from heaven," and we are told by St. Paul, that he is "the same yesterday, to-day, and for ever." Heb. xiii. 8.

IV. OF FORMER BUDDHAS.

As regards existence, Sákya Muni possessed no privilege that is not equally the heritage of all sentient beings. No beginning can be discovered to any person or thing in which there is the principle of life. According to the more definite teachings of Buddha himself, the life that now is never existed before. Indeed, strictly speaking, he admits of no ego; no self or soul; but in referring to the past, the Muni, inconsistently with his other deliverances, makes use of the language common to other systems, and says that in former ages he himself, or some other individual being did certain specified acts.

There have been former Buddhas, but there can be no first Buddha. Beings that are to become Buddhas always existed, and always will. When manifested, they differ in age, stature and caste; but there is no dissidence in the doctrines they teach. In some ages (kalpa) there have been four Buddhas; in others more, and in some only one; but in the present more favoured age there will be five, of whom Sákya Muni was the fourth, and another, who will be called Maitri, has yet to come. By Hodgson the names of 143 Buddhas are given; but he tells us that on one occasion the Muni spoke of 800,000,000 different Buddhas, by all of whom he had himself been instructed. It is frequently affirmed that all knowledge of the Buddhas who existed previously to the last manifestation had passed away; and that all we can now know about them is from the revelations of the sage himself; but these statements are inconsistent with recorded facts, and with other parts of the system. It was a favourite exercise of Sákya Muni to tell the story of former Buddhas, or to listen to a similar recital from the lips of his principal disciples.

V. THE PROMISE.

When compared with the wild assertions of the Dharma in relation to the acts of Sákya Muni and other Buddhas in former states of existence, there is a sobriety, consistency, and grandeur of purpose, in the revelations of the Bible connected with the existence of Christ, before the incarnation that at once commands our sympathy, and our confidence in it as a record of truth. There is on these subjects, a marked reticence in the teachings of our Lord, and we notice the same kind of reserve in the writings of the prophets and apostles. Yet the apostle Peter speaks of Christ as "being foreordained before the foundation of the world, but was manifest in these last times." 1 Peter. i. 20; and he is spoken of by St. John as "the Lamb slain before the foundation of the world." Rev. xiii. 8. It were little to tell the church that God foreknew, or foreordained, the sacrifice of the cross, as "known unto God are all his works from the beginning of the world." Acts. xv. 18; and we must, therefore, conclude that the reference is to solemn and formal occasion, when it was first made known to the hierarchies of heaven, that a Redeemer would be provided for man; who was as yet uncreated, but in after ages to be formed in the divine likeness, and then to fall from his first estate. This conclusion is confirmed by a passage in the fortieth Psalm, ver. 7, where we learn from a vision of heaven that a Redeemer was sought for man, but none was found, until "the everlasting Son of the Father" said, "Lo,

I come, to do Thy will, O God," Heb. x. 7, and then the promise was written in the volume of the book and remained as one of the great traditions of the celestial host. There are other passages in the Psalms, xiv. 6, cx. 4, in which the Son is represented as being addressed by the Father, and the dignity of the priestly office he has to assume acknowledged. We have the authority of St. Paul for affirming that the divine Person here spoken of is the Lord's Christ.—Heb i. 8: v. 6. Before the song was heard in the riven sky above the hill side where the shepherds of Bethlehem fed their flocks, the angel Jehovah had appeared to the ancient dwellers in the same land, as the Messenger of the Covenant; and we learn from Malachi, iii. 1, that the Messenger was manifested as Jesus Christ, "whose goings forth have been from of old, from the days of eternity." Micah v. 2. We are only permitted to see these things now "through a glass, darkly," and must wait for the hour of a revelation. We know enough to give us an instructive, insight into "the analogy of faith;" but the vain curiosity is repressed that would seek to intrude further into this mystic region.

VI. THE PERIOD.

Guided by the voice of the Scriptures, we acknowledge the proper and perfect divinity of Jesus Christ, that he is "over all, God blessed for ever," "from everlasting to everlasting." But here as elsewhere, when away from the record, we enter upon questions connected with infinity and eternity, we are at once in mazes lost; wandering away in the dark, with no object before us upon which the mind can rest; as if we realized nonentity, and yet lived. We can think; but our thoughts seem incapable of being conveyed in the definite terms of speech. Words lose their meaning, and we can only utter them with the consciousness that what we say is unreal, As we thus reflect, we are prompted to ask, "When did it first enter into the mind of God to resolve upon providing a ransom for mankind?" But eternity knows no "when." There is no answer to our question; there can be none. We may be able to tell why the advent of "Him who was to come," the promised One, was delayed so many thousand years. History presents reasons why the incarnation should have been at the particular period when it actually took place. It was "the fullness of time," the era spoken of as "the ends of the world," as to its mediatorial economy; the parenthesis when the separated nations were made to run into each other by the fusion of conquest, so as to form one grand and far extended realm, with a unity of pursuit and purpose that the world had never previously seen. But as to the reason why our earth was created "in the beginning" and not before, or at what time there was the first annunciation of God's love for his creature, man, or under what circumstances the thought of providing an atonement for him was formed in the divine mind; these are mysteries that we are without the means of explaining, as we have no access to the records of heaven, and the way of the Infinite is hid from finite comprehension. It is sufficient for us to know that we have the oath of God to assure us that He has "no pleasure in the death of the wicked, but that the wicked turn from his way and live." Ezek. xxxiii. 11; and that "God so loved the world that He gave His only begotten Son, that whosoever believeth in Him should not perish, but have everlasting life." John iii. 16.

VII. THE WISH.

The more dreamy seems here to be the more definite; but it is only in appearance. Were we able to form characters upon the face of the blue sky, as it extends in its vastness from horizon to horizon, it would be possible to calculate, from the given data on the myriads of ages that elapsed between the period when a sentient being in one of the worlds then existing, after their own manner, formed the resolution to enter upon the course that would end in his becoming a supreme Buddha, and the night in which this wish was realized, under a bô-tree in the Indian forest. According to the Pitakas, when the world has entered upon a period in which wickedness universally prevails, there are none to pass after death into the superior heavens, and they become comparatively empty, as their former inhabitants, from their appointed term of residence in these having expired, have migrated to other states of existence. Long ages ago, one of the dwellers therein, finding the universe in this position, and knowing that no one but a Buddha could bring to it the hope of deliverance, looked everywhere for the intelligence who would be most likely to become an aspirant for the office; and when he had discovered the being for whom he sought, he awoke within him a feeling of pity for the erring and the helpless, and then the thought of becoming their deliverer. The act that attracted attention towards this being was one that bespoke strong affection as well as the possession of much courage and determined resolution. He and his mother were wrecked in a storm at sea, when the future Buddha, supporting his parent, swam towards the shore, amidst sharks and other monsters, by which he succeeded in saving her life. This was the period when he first formed the wish to become "the teacher of the three worlds."

This wish was cherished during the successive existence of 123,000, Buddhas. There was then the expression of the wish during the existence of 387,000 Buddhas; after which he received an assurance from the twenty-four Buddhas who subsequently appeared that he would be their successor.

These periods appear to have no foundation in fact. They are not astronomical cycles, nor are they the exaggeration of a series of historical eras. They are purely imaginary; but the vast and marvellous extent of time that they shadow forth adds to the reverence with which the Buddhists regard the sage in whose words they place their religious trust, as they suppose him to have been seeking, during all this incomprehensible period, the benefit of sentient existence.

CHAPTER II.

THE PURPOSE AND PREPARATION.

I. TRANSGRESSION. II. THE ATONEMENT. III. SAKYA MUNI'S PREVIOUS BIRTHS AND THEIR INFLUENCE. IV. THE CONTRAST.

I. TRANSGRESSION.

There came disorder into the universe when there came the existence of sin. The time must have been when "God saw everything," without exception or limit, "that He had made, and behold it was very good." In every part of creation, all was then subjectively pure and objectively beautiful. The manner of the worlds first marring or the time when, we are not told; but it is the divine decree, co-extensive with intelligent creation, that "the soul that sinneth shall die." By a strong anthropomorphism, the Lord represents himself as grieved when his creatures commit iniquity; "grieved at His heart" The particular circumstances connected with the antemundane rebellion have not been revealed; but we are permitted to learn something of its terrible consequences. The "everlasting fire" was "prepared for the devil and his angels." Matt. xxv. 41. "The angels which kept not their first estate, but left their own habitation, He hath reserved in everlasting chains under darkness unto the judgment of the great day." Jude. 6. Yet never, for a moment, has the song of the seraphim been intermitted, "Holy, holy, holy, is the Lord of hosts;" and if we could learn the whole of the events connected with the expulsion of the fallen angels from heaven, we should doubtless see that the love of God was throughout as clearly displayed as the righteousness of God, and that their punishment is as just as that of finally impenitent men.

II. THE ATONEMENT.

There are difficulties involved in the remission of sin, without an infringement of the justice of God. If possible at all, it must be in some manner consistent with reverence for the divine authority. The majesty of the divine law has to be asserted; and "the wrath of God" appeased. The pardon of the transgressor cannot be by a simple gratuitous act; nor can it be by an all-comprehensive amnesty. From neither of these courses could man on earth have learnt "the exceeding sinfulness of sin;" and other intelligences, from man's impunity, might have been tempted to commit iniquity, thoughtlessly, and fearlessly, under the supposition that no evil of permanent consequence would follow. Nor can the present or the future atone for the past, when even perfection of service is no more than is rightfully required. But in the appointment and acceptance of an atonement of infinite worth, when the iniquities of us all were laid by the divine hand upon Jesus Christ; when the sword that was awoke by the Lord of Hosts was uplifted against the fellow of the Lord of Hosts; when, in the hour of His utmost agony, with His sweat, as great drops of blood falling to the ground, He still said, "Thy will be done"; it was seen that a plan had been devised, and its purpose accomplished, by which God could be "faithful and just to forgive us our sins:" and the same infinitely gracious act became at once the greatest proof of the divine holiness, and of God's earnestness of desire that man should be saved. By the atonement of the Son, the love of the Father was not increased in any degree: but through its influence it became possible for the triune Lord God, without the infringement of any of the divine attributes, leaving them still in the infinity of their perfection, to offer pardon to all men, who will accept it upon the terms on which it can now be righteously presented.

III. SAKYA MUNI'S PREVIOUS BIRTHS AND THEIR INFLUENCE.

Though Buddhism has no right understanding of the guilt of sin, in the antecedents given to Sákya Muni it confesses the necessity of some power not in the possession of ordinary mortals before man can learn the way of release from the consequence of his acts. It offers no help that will impart strength in weakness, but it professes to give instruction to the ignorant and the word of guidance to those who err.

From the time of his call to the Buddhaship incomprehensibly distant, until his appearance in Magadha, Sákya Muni, in each of the myriad existences through which he passed, excelled in one or other of the ten primary virtues —alms-giving, obedience, abandonment of the world, instruction of the ignorant, courage, forbearance, truthfulness, resolution, kindness, or equanimity. Many hundreds of stories are given in proof of his fulfilment of these obligations. In illustration of his kindness, it is said that he sacrificed himself so many times, in his various births, in order to become food for hungry lions, tigers, and demons, and thus prevent them from perishing; that he gave for this purpose more eyes than there are stars in the heavens, more blood than there is water in the four oceans, and more flesh than there is earth in all the continents of the world. In the Chariya Pitaka, in which he gives an account of his previous states of existence, he relates the story of numerous instances of alms-giving, in one of which he collected the sticks, kindled a fire, and cooked himself that he might give his skin, flesh, tendons, and bones to be eaten. At the conclusion he says, "All this was done that I might become a Buddha." In his penultimate birth, he resigned his kingdom with all its treasures and retired to the forest, when he gave his own children in alms to an ascetic who asked them from him; and this was only a repetition of what he had done in other states of existence. These tales may be read with interest, as eastern stories, or as illustrating the manner and customs of former times in India, and some of them may be founded on actual occurrence; but in the greater portion we can discover neither aim nor instructiveness.

To uphold the dignity of the Buddha throughout these births, we are told that he never existed as an insect, or as any small or insignificant animal: nor was he ever defective in any of the senses, or subject to any loathsome disease: nor was he ever a sceptic: the greater sins he always avoided: and he was never a sprite or a demon.

In the earliest of the mystic ages in which Sákya Muni is made to appear as an individual personage, he might have attained Nirvána, and thus have secured freedom from all sorrow and suffering for ever: but out of pity for the various orders of sentient existence, that he might by his teachings release them from the misery to which they are subjected by repeated births, he voluntarily chose to remain in the stream of continued existence, and still to live, and migrate from form to form. But he always avoided being born in any world where his stay would have had to be prolonged, or in which there would be no opportunity for the exercise of the virtues that must unceasingly be exerted by one who aspires to the Buddhaship. It was usually in the world of men that he appeared, though not always as a human being.

There can be no attainment of Nirvána, except by an attention to the truths revealed by a Buddha. After long intervals, regularly and necessarily recurring, a time arrives when, through the perversity of all the sentient beings then in existence, ignorance begins everywhere to prevail, and all rememberance of the truths that have been taught by the Buddhas is lost. It is the great object of a postulant for the Buddhaship to gain the power that will enable him to recover the knowledge that has thus perished. This is all that he can effect in behalf of those whom he seeks to benefit. He can impart no grace: but he can point out to them the path by which they may successfully seek its equivalent. He is, in no sense, man's substitute or atonement: but he proclaims to him the peril attendant upon acts of demerit, and the advantage of following an opposite course. The most precious distinction that he can arrive at is, that he may become a guide to the path by which final release may be gained from all that is connected with "impermanency, sorrow, and unreality." To secure this high position he passes through existences numberless, in many of which his privations and sufferings are of the most appalling kind: but he willingly submits even to the most painful, with expressions of satisfaction and joy, from the prospect presented to him of ultimately becoming the unerring revealer of the paths that lead to rest.

The entire character of the course predicated of Sákya Muni in his pre-existent state is an instructive comment on the Buddhistic ideas of the helplessness of man as a moral agent. It is strongly illustrative of the unrest under which all live, who are of woman born, and of their earnest longing for a state of repose. Whilst the necessity of an atonement by substitution is unacknowledged, the thought itself runs through the whole tissue of the wondrous fable: and as it is seen that no intelligence, according to the principles assumed, can perform so great a work as to render him, worthy to present a sacrifice that would avail for the salvation of others, this lack is sought to be supplied by multiplied repetition of wise and virtuous acts, that, when taken separately, would be confessedly inadequate for the purpose, but when presented in the mighty aggregate seem to have an excellence beyond all possible estimate. The conception is one of the noblest ever formed in the heathen mind, that a sentient being should voluntarily suffer during myriads of ages for the sake of misguided men. But when we remember that it is a mere phantasy, we can only admire the inventiveness of the imagination whence it sprang, and acknowledge how much there is about it that would seem, if it were a reality, to meet the great desiderata of a wailing universe.

IV. THE CONTRAST.

In the Son of God there was all the pity for man that by the Dharma is falsely attributed to Buddha. With the divine Redeemer there was no actual suffering until the time of his reception of the manhood, but there was a perfection of foresight in relation to all that was afterwards to be endured that no finite mind can comprehend. The victim reeking upon the patriarchal altar was a frequent remembrance presented before the throne, of the promise made previous to the foundatian of the world. The command given to the man of God to offer up his only son, in the same region in which the real sacrifice was afterwards to be slain; the inspired words he was enabled to speak, at the most painful moment of his trial, "The Lord will provide;" the service of the priesthood, constantly presented in the tabernacle; the burden of such Psalms as the twenty-second, sung daily in the temple; and the revelations of the prophets, more particularly of Isaiah terribly graphic, in which there is a crowded grouping of the the scenes of agony, through which the Redeemer would have to pass in his last hours, were all significant in their utterance, and seemed to repeat unceasingly the word of troth spoken to the Father, "Lo, I come." The glorious character of the Mediator, the infinity of the distance between Him who came and those for whom he came; the greatness of the antecedent abnegation, when He who possessed the riches of the universe, "emptied Himself" and became poor, a homeless wanderer, that the rebels against His authority, "through His poverty might be rich:" the unutterable anguish that He endured when there was wrung from His dying lips, in this hour of darkness, the mysterious exclamation, "My God, My God, why hast Thou forsaken Me?" bring home to us, since Christ came, in still clearer and brighter characters, the limitless grandeur of the heart-solacing truth, "God is Love," and illustrate the constraining activity and indomitable strength of our Lord's merciful resolve to accomplish the salvation of the world.

CHAPTER III.*

THE INCARNATION.

Whatever may have been the origin of the thought, there can be no doubt that there was a wide-spread expectation, about the time of the advent of Jesus Christ, that some great King was about to arise in the east who would attain to universal dominion. The first intimation of the near approach of this event was in the appearance of the angel Gabriel to the aged Zachariah, as he was exercising the priest's office in the temple at Jerusalem He was told that his wife Elizabeth would bear a son at whose birth many would rejoice as he would "go before (the Lord their God) in the spirit and power of Elias" Six months afterwards, the same angel appeared to Mary, a virgin then resident at Nazareth, in humble circumstances, though of the royal house of David, from whom she learnt that without knowing man, through the agency of the Holy Ghost, she would conceive and bring forth a son, and that because of "the overshadowing of the power of the Highest," He who was to be born of her should be called the Son of God.

These are the more important of the circumstances that have been revealed concerning the miraculous conception. The manner in which the virgin became a mother is thus told us in terms the most unaffected; and yet they are sufficiently precise to assure us of the fulfilment of the prophecy which foretold that the seed of the woman should bruise the serpent's head. Gen iii. 15, Through the veil of purity that invested Mary, we are permitted to mark her entire submissiveness to the will of God, as she timidly, but trustfully, listens to the strange words spoken to her by the messenger from heaven.

---

* From this chapter the headings of paragraphs are not inserted in the MS.

The scene of the annunciation has called forth the utmost skill of some of the noblest painters that the world ever produced; but we are perplexed by the multitude of their Madonnas; and there is an image revealed to the thoughtful soul that surpasses in gentle grace and calm dignity, the most successful product of the easel

"When the fulness of time was come, God sent forth His Son made of a woman, made under the law, to redeem them that were under the law, that we might receive the adoption of sons." Gal. iv. 4. The Scriptural record of the birth of Christ is too quiet and unpretending to be an invention. "There were shepherds abiding in the fields keeping watch over their flocks by night." The pasture-ground of these favoured men was nigh to "Bethlehem, the city of David." It might be, that they had been conversing together on the extreme beauty of the words written by one who had there kept a similar night-watch in the days of his youth; and of the glorious scenes that he had afterwards been permitted to sketch, under the guidance of the Holy Spirit, in relation to the King who "shall deliver the needy when he crieth; the poor also, and him that hath no helper:" and when their hearts were full of rapture at the joyous thought, they may have broken out into holy song, and made the hills around re-echo with the concluding words of the same Psalm, in which is presented the uttermost wish-thought of a devout spirit, "Let the whole earth be filled with His glory." They might have heard the common report that the Messiah was to be expected about this time; and have remembered the prophecy that he was to be born in their own land, and have said to each other, "How glorious if it were now!" Suddenly, there was with the angel a multitude of the heavenly host, praising God and saying, "Glory to God in the highest, and on earth peace, good-will to men" On the departure of the celestial visitants, the shepherds came to Bethlehem, where they found the new-born Child, lying in a manger, "because there was no room for them in the inn." This was "Christ, the Lord." The inspired physician who pens this narrative, does it with the same calmness as that with which he writes out the tabulated genealogy of our Lord. We are led by it to infer that not a single inhabitant of the adjacent city was awoke by the song, and that no warden keeping watch on the towers of Jerusalem, saw the angelic glory. The entire spirit of the scene is thus in strong contrast with the record of the spurious gospels; and with the events said to have been connected with the birth of nearly all the personages of fiction to whom divinity is ascribed.

It is regarded as essential, that the Buddhas possess the human nature, and that they be of woman-born. Otherwise, the marvellous acts that they perform might be attributed to an influence that they share in common with celestial intelligences. They would then be looked on as deities inheriting supernatural power by means of their divine origin, and not as beings who have attained to perfection in wisdom and supremacy in power, by a long course of noble and virtuous deeds. It was thought that by the accomplishment of the unparallelled course through which he had passed, Sákya Muni had acquired the right to become an authoritative teacher, superseding and setting aside, all other instructors. It was this alleged superiority, that was supposed to give men an assurance that the faith they exercise in the Dharma he taught rests upon an immovable basis.

The preparation for the final birth of Buddha was witnessed by the residents of the heaven in which he lived rather than by men upon earth. Like the dew resting upon the smooth stem of a tree in the forest, his body was seen to exude moisture, and the ornaments of his person began to fade and become dim. At an auspicious moment, he left his place in heaven, and entered the human world as the child of Suddhódana and Máya, the king and queen of Kapilavastu, a city of Northern India, the exact site of which has not been ascertained. There are many statements in the native books, the tendency of which is, to suggest the idea of the virginity of the beautiful Máya at the time of his birth, and it is said that seven days afterwards she died. This notion is strongly insisted on by the Mongols,* but it is not taught explicitly by the southern Buddhists or by the Tibetans. It must have prevailed more generally in the fifth century, as Jerome says, that Buddha was believed to have been born of a virgin, and to have come from his mother's side.

Though the character of Máya is presented to us as spotless, and she is invested with every feminine attribute that can command respect, and all the glory that the oriental imagination can invent is thrown around her, she has no place among the objects of worship received by the Buddhists. They have too much veneration for the sage through whom they seek to be taught the way of truth, to share his honour even with

* Schmidt quoting a Mongol legend says, "*Il entra, sous la forme d'un rayon de lumiere de cinq couleurs, dans le sein de la reine Maha Máya.*" Foé Koué Ki. 223

this most virtuous of women, whom they compare to "the casket that has held the most precious jewel that ever dazzled the vision of men." This may partly arise from the low estimate in which women are regarded in almost every part of the east; but in this abstinence they have shewn more discretion and greater propriety than the Greek and Latin churches, by whom Mary, regarded with a morbid feeling, in which sensuousness and superstition equally mingle, is worshipped as the queen of heaven. When the predicted outpouring of the Spirit shall come, the Mariolatry of this and preceding ages will be contemplated with the utmost astonishment and indignation.

The moment of the assumption of humanity by Buddha was marked by the appearance of a light that illumined all worlds, and by many wonders still more incredible. Until his birth, Brahma and other deities kept watch around the couch of his mother. At the end of the appointed months, when on the way to visit the home of her parents, who resided at a city not far distant, she resolved to rest during the heat of the day in a pleasant garden, through which she had to pass; and whilst in this place, listening to the hum of bees and inhaling the fragrance of numberless flowers, her son, Sákya Muni, was born A friendly tree bent its boughs around her, and formed a screen that hid her from the observation of her attendants; and the future sage was brought forth in purity and without pain. The prince of the deities, Brahma, received the long-hoped-for child upon a golden net-work. By him the precious treasure was delivered to the divine guardians of the four quarters, and by them to the nobles of the palace, who gave him to the royal nurses. The Muni at once stepped upon the ground, and after looking in every direction, said "I am the most exalted in the world: I am chief in the world: I am the most excellent in the world: hereafter, I shall not receive another birth." When presented by the king to his chief counsellor, that aged minister worshipped him, and declared his future greatness.

As thus presented, the advent of Sákya Muni can have few parallels among other incarnations. It was not an *avatár*, like that of the Hindu gods These became men, and walked the earth, still retaining their divinity, though they appeared for a time under another guise; and when the purpose had been fulfilled for which they visited our world, they returned to their former position. But it is not thus with the Buddhas. When they die, their being ceases; they have no further existence; the voice of the instructor is thenceforth silent for ever.

It has been supposed that the idea of incarnation is so familiar to the Hindus, that they are prepared at once to receive the teaching of Scripture, that "God was manifest in the flesh;" but the missionaries tell us that they are sometimes asked by the natives, "How could God become incarnate?"* From this it would seem that we have been much mistaken as to the form in which this mystery appears to the Hindu mind, and have transferred to them our own notions upon the subject, founded upon revelation. We have been wrong in applying to these the precision of cultivated thought. As regards all psychological speculation, there is vagueness in their minds, connected with impressions that to us appear utterly childish. Naturalness, or congruity of sequence, forms no part of their dialectics. Among mankind, the sex may be changed, even in adult life, from the male to the female and from the female to the male. Nágas, whose proper shape is that of the serpent, may assume the human form, and procreate children by human mothers. Among the gods, one deity may have a multiplicity of forms at the same time, as in the case of the five Pándavas, who were said by the sage Vyása to be five incarnations of India, "and consequently the same as one man."† But the acts attributed to the gods are, in many instances, reduced to a seeming, and are not regarded as a reality even by the chroniclers of their deeds.

Whilst the Buddhists are anxious, for the reasons they assign, to prove the humanity of Sákya Muni, there have been heresiarchs in the church who have taught, less wisely, that the human nature of our Lord was in appearance only, his body not having a real existence; so that he had divinity without humanity, and did not possess a human soul. It was in reference to a similar error that the apostle John said, "Many deceivers are entered into the world, who confess not that Jesus Christ is come in the flesh. This is a deceiver and an antichrist." 2 John. 7. The heterodox notion arose from the belief that all matter is inherently and necessarily connected with contamination But the church is taught that Jesus Christ is "perfect man," as well as "perfect God;" "of a reasonable soul and human flesh subsisting;" and that "two whole and perfect natures, that is to say, the Godhead and the manhood were joined together in one person, never to be divided, whereof is one Christ, very God and very Man." Unless

---

* Chronicle of the London Missionary Society, 1867:

† Wheeler's Maha Bhárata, 134.

we receive this doctrine in its unbroken simplicity, that the divine Logos was made flesh, a great part both of the Old Testament and the New is without meaning, and we are "yet in our sins." It was because the blood that was shed for our redemption was the blood of man, human blood in which was human life, that it became a homoousian substitute for mankind; and it was because the same blood, through the hypostatic union, was "the blood of God" (or as some readings say, of the Lord), that on being shed it became a sacrifice of infinite worth and unlimited efficacy. In the humanity perfect, in the Divinity equally perfect, our Redeemer was nevertheless one Christ; so that in the union of the two natures there is neither confusion nor conversion; though there is one volition, manifested in perfect oneness of operation. The manner of this union we cannot explain, as we cannot explain how the body and soul form one man.

CHAPTER IV.

THE EARLY LIFE.

We are again reminded, by the absence of all extravagance in the records we receive from the sacred historians, that we are still called upon to deal with the realities of sober truth, and not with the fancies of the poet or the sensational incidents of romance. We are simply told of the child Jesus, in addition to the visit of the shepherds, that Herod, the king, sought his life; he was circumcised, and received a name descriptive of his office and work; he was presented in the temple, when the venerable Simeon was there, who was "waiting for the consolation of Israel;" wise men from the further east offered to him gifts, consisting of gold, frankincense, and myrrh; he and his mother were taken to Egypt, that they might be safe from the murderous designs of the crime-haunted monarch; he dwelt in a city called Nazareth; he "grew and waxed strong in spirit, filled with wisdom, and the grace of God was upon him." There is here no straining after effect; no detail of prodigies attendant upon the youth of whom so high a destiny had been predicted. Nearly every incident we have named might have occurred to any peasant of the same land. Assuring dreams, the appearance of a star, and the message and song of the heavenly host, are the only events of a purely supernatural character. At an early age the word of God must have been his constant study. We know that he read and wrote; and when, at twelve years of age, he sat in the temple, in the midst of the doctors, "both hearing them and asking questions," we are certain, from the place of the assembly, from the known studies of the learned men, whom he encountered, and his own character, that the questions he himself asked, whatever might be the form of those he was called upon to answer, were founded upon subjects connected with his "Father's business," the elevated nature of which he had learnt from the fountain of inspiration. The teachers of the east did not confine themselves to the formal address of the lecture room. They were ready to meet all comers in the arena of controversy; and in proportion to the readiness and skill exhibited on these occasions was the renown of the rabbi or the pundits. The only thing in the position taken by Christ, that would appear to be out of the usual course, would arise from his youth, and from the wisdom shewn in the answers he gave; which would be the more marked, from the contrast they presented to the platitudes and puerilities of which the Mishna and the Talmud were afterwards the perfected efflorescence.

At this time, it was the custom of Jesus to attend the religious festivals appointed in the law; and we are told that he was "subject to them," i. e. his parents, to Joseph as well as to Mary. The great lesson of "obedience" that he had to learn, and by which he was made "made perfect," had already commenced, to be carried on and consummated in the more terrible discipline of a later period, when "he offered up prayers, and supplications, with strong crying and tears, unto Him that was able to save him from death." Increasing alike "in wisdom and stature," or age, *helikia*, with the increase of bodily strength there was an increase also in the capacity and power of the mind, and in its endowments. From the question, "Is not this the carpenter?" asked in "his own country," by those who must have known him well, we may suppose that he had personally worked by the side of Joseph's bench; unless it were a kind of caste name that was given him, in reference to the trade of his reputed father rather than to labour wrought out by his own hand. The favour with which he was regarded by God rested upon him in an increasing degree, to be more openly manifested at a later period of his life, when, amidst a radiance that overpowered the senses of the disciples that were with him, so that they wist not what they spake, the voice of the Father said, "This is my beloved Son, in whom I am well pleased."

The increase of favour was not only with God, but "with man." From this expression we receive an instructive insight into the manner of the life of Jesus whilst resident at Nazareth.

It was in perfect contrast to that of John. We read not that the son of Zechariah was ever called a craftsman, nor have we any hint that he ever engaged in manual labour or learnt any art; though this course was then customary even among the Jews that were brought up to the study of the law. "He was in the deserts till the day of his shewing unto Israel." Wandering in solitude; living on locusts that he might catch with his own hand as "they marched every one on his own way," without breaking their ranks, and on honey that he gathered from the cleft of the rock near which he lay as the jackal prowled around; and clothed in a rough dark garment of camel's hair, he was regarded by the people with awe; and as they whispered to each other of his strange ways, they said, "He hath a devil." On the other hand, Jesus Christ lived in the midst of the domestic circle, probably working at a trade, and he frequented the synagogue on the sabbath. From what travellers have told us of the locality we may fancy ourselves tracing his footsteps We now see him at the door of the carpenter's dwelling, with the sacred scroll in his hand, which he attentively reads, as the turtle-dove murmurs, and the breeze rustles, among the fronds of the palm-tree above him, or the shades of evening throw around the sombre olive-trees growing near an air of still deeper pensivness; we now watch him as he treads the bank of the mountain rill, which trickles and foams in its hurried rushing toward the cultivated plain of Esdrælon; and we now accompany him as his eye glances over the rich and varied scenery that is commanded by many a spot within an easy walk from the gate of Nazareth. By all he is regarded with respect; and the more pious of the neighbours look on him with bright anticipations of an undefined future. And yet there are evidences of deep thoughtfulness, and the foreshadowing of that look of sadness which was seen in still greater sorrow when "his visage was marred more than any man," and they who saw him "did esteem him stricken, smitten of God, and afflicted." But in the midst of all this subduedness of manner, there was so much gentleness and goodness, so strong an attractiveness in the way of his every-day life, that though it must have been known among the other villages that there awaited him some high and important place in the kingdom of God, so far from envy being at this time excited, or a spirit of jealousy aroused, we have evidence that he was regarded with favour by the dwellers in this secluded nook of Galilee. He had favour with man, as well as with God, and in that favour there was an increase day by day.

We have prolix accounts of the childhood and youth of Sákya Muni; but all that is said of his early life, is so essentially different to the picture presented of Christ by the evangelists, and is in itself so unhistorical and untruthful, that we should hesitate to notice it at all, were it not that the scenes of Nazareth are not only dissimilar, in their entire voice and vision, from the acts ascribed to the prince of Mágadha, but also in perfect contrast, we repeat, with what is told us of any other person who has founded a religion or become an object of worship; so that were the facts given in connexion with the early biography of Jesus placed side by side with any of the legends to which we refer, it would at once be seen, without any collateral argument, which is the record of truth. The future Buddha was nursed by a thousand princesses. The architect of the gods prepared for him a magnificent bath. When five months old, he sat in the air, without any visible support, and as his retinue gathered together in wonder, and offered him worship, the sun so ordered its rays that the tree above threw around him a vertical shadow. When it was intended to appoint his court, from the habits he was known to have formed, he was regarded as a weak and spiritless youth, a mere student, an object of pity rather than of pride, and there was difficulty in filling up his zenána from the royal families of the province. But to convince the reluctant princes that they were wrong in the estimate they had formed of his character, in the presence of vast multitudes he drew a bow with the greatest ease that a thousand men could not bend, and blind-folded he shot an arrow with so sure an aim, that it severed a hair from which a small object was suspended in the distance. With another arrow he pierced, in one flight, four trees that were planted at each corner of a square.

It had been predicted that he would become a Buddha. This was against the wish of his father, who intended that he should ascend the throne and reign as king, surrounded by splendour and state. To prevent the issue that he so much dreaded, the monarch surrounded his son by objects that were designed to allure him to a life of pleasure and dissipation; and guards were placed around him that were to prevent the approach of any object, or the occurrence of any event, that might tend to lead his mind in a contrary direction. But these precautions were in vain. He saw, at intervals, when seated in his chariot, first a loathsome leper, then an emaciated old man, a dead body, on its way to the grave-yard, and a religious mendicant. The sight of the three objects of distress gave him a clear insight into the vanity of every thing existent, and the becoming deportment of the ascetic having inspired him with an intense desire to embrace a religious life, the resolution was formed that at the first opportunity which presented itself he would abandon the world Not long afterwards the apearance of the palace after a night of revelry, with the festive garlands faded, every thing in disorder, the attendants jaded, all around sad and silent, and the courtezans, robbed of all attractiveness and grace, either listlessly yawning or asleep, confirmed him in the resolution he had made. When a festival was held in honour of the birth of his son, as his guards relaxed their vigilance, after taking a farewell look of the mother and her babe, who were placidly sleeping at the time, he mounted a horse, and without telling any one of his intention, fled away into the forest, where, after proceeding many miles, he commanded the attendant to take the animal back to the palace. He then cut off his hair, and assumed the garb of a mendicant, and visiting the city of Rajagaha, he proceeded from house to house with the alms-bowl in search of food. Though it was of the commonest description, he ate what he received meditatively, reflecting on its impurities, to which he compared the elements and secretions of which his own body was composed. From this time, he was never known to laugh; though sometimes seen to smile. Five Brahmans accompanied him in the performance of the ascetic exercises he now began to practice, but as he had not obtained the Buddhaship after the penance of six years, in which he gradually reduced the quantity of food he ate, until he lived upon a single pepper corn daily, they left him, and went to reside on the city of Benares.

We have here presented only the residuum of a vast mass of incidents with which the infancy and youth of Sákya Muni are invested in the Asiatic biographies. It would be easy to form from them an instructive narrative, but there would be no reliance upon it as a record of fact. Resident in a palace, married at the age of sixteen years to a beautiful and virtuous princess, possessed of every advantage that could be supposed to afford the means of happiness or give zest to life, his mind was still far from being at rest; he found that what are called the pleasures of the world were agitating and unsatisfactory, and he longed for the peace that he thought solitude, and opportunity for meditation, would bring to his perturbed spirit. He did not retain possession of wealth and power until compelled to relinquish them by political reverses or the approach of old age. It was in the hey-day of his manhood that he resigned them, and became a wanderer in the wilderness. This supposed example, presenting the kind of attractiveness best calculated to influence the thoughtful eastern mind, would be made prominent in the discourses of his disciples, when they sought to persuade men to join their fraternity and assume the alms-bowl.

The public ministry of Jesus Christ commenced when "he began to be about thirty years of age." Sákya Muni fled from the attractions of the palace when twenty-nine years of age; but he remained in the solitudes of the forest seven years before he gained the Buddhaship, and proclaimed himself as the unerring teacher. The preparation of the Muni for the exercise of this office was by acts of penance, severe and long-continued; but the Messiah, from the earliest dawn of reason, had the grace of God resting upon him, and was taught of the Spirit. At the baptism in Jordan, the Holy Ghost came down upon him visibly, and probably in greater measure; in that limitless fulness which is said to have been "without measure." There are many circumstances connected with the history of Christ. The meaning of which will be inexplicable, unless we constantly bear in mind the primal truth that he became manifest in order that the Lord might lay upon him "the iniquity of us all," and that he made him to be "sin for us who knew no sin." It, therefore, behoved him, under this idea, "to fulfil all righteousness;" to pass through all those forms of ceremonial observance, and all those phases of mental exercise, that are meted out to the sinner *de facto*, though he himself was "without sin." He who had been circumcised, though he needed it not; and "as his custom was" went into the synagogue on the Sabbath day, though all the angels of God were called upon to worship him; and attended the festival of the passover, though he himself was the divine antitype of the slain lamb; now received baptism at the hands of John, though he wanted no lustration by water, and was himself the "greater than John." A further design was accomplished by his attendance upon the rite. The prophets, in ancient times, had foretold many things that were descriptive of his manner and mission; but it had been declared to John, "Upon whom thou shalt *see* the Spirit descending from heaven, and remaining on him, the same is he which baptizeth with the Holy Ghost." It must have been consolatory to the mind of John, and a confirmation of his faith in him that was to come, as he still abode in the wilderness, honoured by thousands of his country-men, but his life sought by the monarch who at last cast him into prison and then put him to death. But he was permitted to see with his own eyes his kinsman Jesus, of whom his mother must have told him many a tale of wonder when he dwelt at home, preparing for the high position he was about to assume as "the forerunner of the Lord." If he had had any doubts previously as to the supreme dignity of his relative they were removed by the attesting voice of God, and the visible descent upon him of the Holy Ghost, whether it was, as some suppose, literally in the shape of a dove, or as others think, with the hovering fluttering motion of the dove when about to fold its wings and alight. To Jesus himself, at the commencement of his ministry, the same tokens were not without an important significance. The Jews were prepared for the present appearance of some one of the house of Israel through whom the Lord would perform the oath he had sworn to their father Abraham. The seers of old had said that he would come, and the aged Simeon had said he was come; and though the multitude knew not of the word spoken in the temple there was a general belief that the time of the nation's deliverance was at hand. This we learn from St Luke: "The people were in expectation and all men mused in their hearts of John, whether he was the Christ or not." When John declared that one mightier than himself would come, the latchet of whose shoes he was not worthy to unloose, their musings would be turned away from the Baptist and go out in search of the Mighty One whose advent had been so long foretold. It was, therefore, to the Jews a strong proof of the Messiahship of Jesus, when the divinely appointed messenger could say of him, that he had seen and heard the sealing of the Father, made known to him under circumstances that left no doubt as to the divinity of its origin; and when under the impulse of the same power he could say, with uplifted hand, "Behold the Lamb of God that taketh away the sin of the world," it was clearly seen that He of whom the prophets spoke was in their midst.

The consecration of Sákya Muni to the Buddhaship was not attended by any similar act. For years he sought in vain the requisite power and attainments, until his companions, wearied out by repeated disappointment, left him to pursue the further search alone. It was his office to teach, and not to "take away sin;" and we have no reference to any such initiatory rite as that of baptism.

CHAPTER V.

THE TEMPTATION.

The oldest prophecy contained in the word of God relative to the Messiah, and the one that is almost more comprehensive and more perfectly descriptive, than any other taken separately of the work he would come to accomplish is contained in the sentence passed upon the serpent in Eden, "It (the seed of the woman) shall bruise thy head." We have here an agent of evil, called the serpent, possessed of reason, and endowed with speech. His abrupt appearance startles us, as would the rustling of the same reptile, with its rapid movements, and sharply fascinating eye, amidst the crass leaves that lie in our pathway. To tempt man to an act of rebellion against God is his first recorded act. The mental power he possesses tells us that he is no ordinary serpent; and the malignity he exhibits, that he is a spirit of evil. When Christ addressed the unbelieving Jews, he said, "Ye are of your father the devil, and the lusts of your father ye will do. He was a murderer from the beginning." The apostle John twice speaks of "that old serpent, called the devil and Satan, which deceiveth the whole world." By the existence of this being we can account for many a strong and sudden suggestion to do wrong that shoots across the mind of even sincere servants of God; and for the bitterness, and intensity of viciousness, that make some men utterly defiant of all power and authority.

We are prepared, by previous notices of the character of Satan, to learn that all his subtlety was put forth to frustrate the design of the advent of Christ. We know not how far, or with what clearness he saw into the future, when he first tempted men; but we may infer that the great outline of the effects of the fall must have been in some measure understood by the spiritual intelligences then existent; and if this thought be correct, he might have known that his stratagem would succeed for a time, though he might still be ignorant of its present consequences or of its final results. But when he made the assault upon the Redeemer, it must have been with a different anticipation; as the same voice that had foretold the fall of man had made known the triumph of the Son of God. The bruising of the heel had been accomplished; but the more effective and more terrible bruising of the head had yet to come. Warily, with all the forethought that demon spirits can exercise, would the snare be laid, upon the success of which the most important of all issues was to depend. 1 In the insidiousness attendant on the temptation by which the second Adam was assailed, there is some resemblance to that which had succeeded with the first Adam. "Command that these stones be made bread." It was not wrong to eat of the fruit of a tree; He who was afterwards to multiply a few barley loaves and small fishes for the nourishment of hungry thousands, might be supposed, when away from all sustenance, to change the products of the desert into wholesome and convenient food without the transgression of any divine law. The sin consists in the peculiarity of the circumstances The first was a direct infringement of God's positive command; the second would have been an expression of distrust in God. But when tempted to this act, Christ said, quoting the Scripture, "Man shall not live by bread alone, but by every word that proceedeth out of the mouth of God." 2. "Then the devil taketh him up to the holy city, and setteth him on a pinnacle of the temple, and saith unto him, If thou be the Son of God cast thyself down, for it is written, He shall give his angels charge concerning thee; and in their hands they shall bear thee up, lest at any time thou dash thy foot against a stone." Thus Satan, taking ready advantage of the scriptural quotation just made by Christ, sought apparently, to carry out the same thought: "True; thou art specially provided for by the Source of all protective power; then test the reality of that divine guardianship, and put honour upon it, by an open manifestation of thy trust in it as the word of God." To have yielded to this temptation would have been to presume upon the interference of God in a case where there was no necessity for its exercise, and no authority to look for its exhibition, and thus to commit the same evil, under a converse form, that would have been attendant upon yielding to the former suggestion; by presenting an evidence of dissatisfaction with the arrangements of divine Providence, and an unwillingness to submit to the prescribed economy of the Father. It would have been a direct violation of the promise recorded in the volume of the book. "Lo, I come to do thy will, O God." 3. The third count of the temptation was of a similar character. The sin of man consists in a want of acquiescence in the position in which he has been placed by God, leading to a vain endeavour to free himself from the influence of the circumstances that are appointed to be his lot, and to an ambition that prompts him to grasp at things forbidden and make himself lord of whatever presents itself alluring to his senses. In Eden, man wanted to know all things; since his fall, he wants to possess all things. Understanding, as the result of much keen watching, what is man, Satan, in his attempts to ensnare the Messiah, employed a device that had hitherto seldom failed in its exercise. "Again, the devil taketh him up into an exceeding high mountain, and sheweth him all the kingdom of the world, and the glory of them; and saith unto him, All these things will I give thee, if thou wilt fall down and worship me." Here the mask was thrown off, and the climax of the devil's audacity was perfected. There appears to be a morbid anxiety in Satan to receive religious homage from mankind, and in this respect to be "as God." But "hitherto shalt thou go and no further." Christ, who had until now, for our sakes, submitted to the insolence of the adversary, when his words were too audaciously outspoken to be suffered to continue, assumed the majesty of the divine Sonship, and said, "Get thee behind me Satan!" and discomfitting him with the weapon wherewith he had himself presumptuously attempted to conquer, said, "Thou shalt worship the Lord thy God, and him only shalt thou serve." These words were the last sharp arrow drawn from the quiver of God, and must have struck upon his chased spirit as a weapon of mighty power from the hand of the Omnipotent.

All these acts are in perfect keeping with the other revelations of Scripture upon demoniacal subjects. The devil is represented as the great adversary of man, seeking continually to deceive him by his "snares," "devices," and "wiles." There is one evil spirit who is called "the prince of this world," "the prince of the power of the air," "the god of this world;" but confederated in the same league there are unclean intelligences who are "the rulers of the darkness of this world." They were originally happy and holy beings; but they kept not their first estate, and it would appear that it was through pride they forfeited the privileges of the inheritance to which they were created, still retaining for a time a limited or restricted rule. We read "the power of Satan." and we know that in the time of Christ and the earlier Christians, the devils "possessed" men, and not only excited them to do wickedly, but tormented them and inflicted on them sore disease and distress.

We receive the accounts of the temptation in the wilderness in their plain and straightforward meaning, without personification or metaphor, and as recording the acts of a spirit that even now "worketh in the children of disobedience," but who shall be bound, bruised, beaten down, and destroyed by, "the Lord and Giver of life" We also regard the event as an actual occurrence. We may further remark, that as presented in the Gospel narrative, the temptation by which Christ was assailed was of a character entirely different, in many important particulars, from what is recorded of the contests of other minds, with the powers of evil. There is throughout an implied consciousness that it was not a mere man who was assailed; and the record is as remarkable for what it omits as for what it brings forward.

In Buddhism, the existence of an order of beings is taught who are called yakas, but they neither answer to the *daimonioi* of the Greeks nor the devils of Scripture. They are found on the earth, in the waters, and in the heavens. They present various degrees of malignity; and in some instances are free from any greater amount of evil in their dispositions than is predicated of other intelligences. The same beings are at other times regarded as demigods. They are the guardians of the northern quarters of the heaven of Indra; but they are also represented as devouring men when caught in the lonely pool or the unfrequented jungle; and as inhabiting remote islands, where they exercise great cruelty over those who fall within their grasp. Sákya Muni taught a form of exorcism, the repetition of which would prevent their approach to his followers with a sinister design, whether they were "walking, standing, sitting, or reclining." But there is a want of definiteness and uniformity in the accounts we receive of these beings; and it is probable that some of the attributes now given to these were unacknowledged by the Muni, and a belief in their extreme maliciousness may have arisen from an older and more general superstition.

The great opponent of Sákya Muni was Mára, the ruler of the sixth heaven (Déva-loka.) The most determined of his attacks was immediately previous to the reception of the Buddhaship; but it was not so much in the form of a temptation, as in that of a direct assault, with martial weapons of earthly temper, transfered to the hands of beings of supernatural power. No reason is given for the enmity of Mára that might not have been affirmed of any other supreme dêva. The legend tells us that he was afraid lest the ministry of Buddha should impart so much merit to men as to make them worthy of an entrance into a heaven superior to his own, and thus rob him of the homage and fealty of those who would otherwise have been his subjects, and prevent the world he governed from being peopled by its usual number of occupants. We give a rapid sketch of what is said to be recorded in the sacred books. There is too little interest about it to demand a more extended notice.

The first snare intended to place the reception of the Buddhaship by Sákya Muni in peril was brought forward at the time when the prince was forming the design to abandon the world, disgusted with the appearance of the palace after the grand festival held in honour of the birth of his son. Whilst reflecting on this scene, Mára who saw his intention proclaimed to him that if he would forego the search for a knowledge of the Dharma he would receive, in its stead, universal empire, with the honours and riches of all worlds poured at his feet. But he rejected the thought; and as soon might the waters of the Ganges flow back to their source amidst the snows in the forest of the Himalayas, as for such a course to have been taken by the Muni. "Begone! hinder me not," was said by him, as with the voice of a lion, and Mára retired gnashing his teeth with rage. Seven years afterwards, during the whole of which period the opposition of Mára never ceased, the prince said that the hour of victory had come, and he seated himself at the foot of the bo-tree, looking towards the east, that he might prepare for assault. An offering of food presented to him by the daughter of a noble was opportune, as he was afterwards to fast seven times seven days. He was alone; no relative or friend was near him, but there was with him an effectual power of protection derived from the virtues he had practised during myriads of ages, that were in the stead of defensive, weapons or a walled rampart. There were nine several attacks made by Mára; not merely to prevent him from continuing in the new path he had chosen, but to destroy him utterly. They were by wind, rain, rocks, arms, walls of fire, hot ashes, burning sand, mire and filth, and darkness, and in addition, by the hurling of the magical discus. But the sage remained calm and fearless: the blast of the storm was changed into a pleasant breeze, the deluge of rain into gentle dew, the rocks into festive garlands, the arms into lotus flowers, the coals into rich rubies, the sand into pearls, and the darkness into intense radiance. At each fresh attempt, Mára was assisted by serpents with hissing tongues, by beasts of huge size and formidable strength, and by all orders of monsters, and sprites, and demons. But all these efforts were without avail, and when Mára saw that he was conquered, he retired to his own world, and all the dwellers in the celestial spheres came to acknowledge the supremacy of the Muni and rejoice that the Buddhaship had been obtained. On the retreat of Mára, his three daughters, whose names are significant of all that is sensual, sought to seduce the sage by their wiles and wantonness, but he still remained immovable as the crystal rock.*

This Buddhist episode is without consistency, and difficult to explain on any principle that would give it a set purpose, or harmony of action. We have a fierce antagonism, without any adequate reason for its intensity† The Erinnyes of the Greeks, with serpents entwined among their dark hair, are the avengers, and empower the curse to reach the victim, against whom it has been uttered The religious system of the Zoroastians acknowledges the existence of two co-eval principles, the one working what is good in the universe, and the other what is evil. The ancient epics of the Aryans represent the gods as interfering in human affairs, and exhibiting all the hate and envy of this lower world. The early Christian anchorets had to contend with demons, who haunted them in their retirement with every form of enticement and overawing.‡ The scene at the bo-tree, both in the main action, and in the development of the plot diverges so much from the general spirit of the events recorded in other portions of the Pitakas, that we may at once pronounce it to be an interpolation. It is much more in consonance with Brahmanism, from which it must have been derived.

There is the appearance of the daughters of Mára, which must not be overlooked. In the Sanskrit lexicons Mára is

---

* Throughout his life, Mára remained as close to Sákya Muni as his own shadow ; and three months before his death, he tempted the sage to precipitate his entrance into nírvana by trying to persuade him that he had already taught the various orders of sentient beings all that it was necessary for them to learn.

† In all religions with which we are acquainted the existence is acknowledged of an instrumentality supposed to be the cause of man's misfortune, either immediately or as an agent, with which most frequently another power is connected, that seeks to thwart him in the carrying out of his best and noblest purposes.

‡ All these instances of antagonism are in harmony with the systems to which they belong.

said to be a name of Káma, the Hindu Eros; and under this idea the whole may resolve itself into an allegorical contest between purity and sensuality; it represents, in strong terms, the fierceness of the struggle, but there is none of the dangerous seductiveness that the Greeks have thrown around the story of passion. Eros would disdain to use arrows of so rude a shape as those of Mára. But the introduction of the celestial wantons appears to be an afterthought, as if to make up for the strange omission that the being who is represented as the personification of sensuality never once employed this mode of allurement to overcome the resolution of the Muni. Under another form, Mára is represented as the regent of death, as if to make known the extent of his empire, and to teach that all that place themselves under the influence of Mára, as the genius of evil passion, must also submit to Mara as the genius of death. By the Burmans, again the word Mára is said to signify pride, which introduces a new element, more in harmony with the general sentiment of the imagery by which the contest is characterized. These conclusions appear naturally to arise from the Buddhist story, and they may have been present to the mind of the original narrators; but in the native record there appears to be no intimation of anything beyond the bald literal meaning, and the stolid writers seem ignorant that any moral is to be learnt therefrom beside the simple fact of the superiority of the Muni to the Mára.

In the presentation of the glories of the universe and their rejection, in the fasting connected with the trial and in the period of its duration; in the malignity of the opposing agent; in the majesty with which the command to depart was given; in the vehement longing for supremacy exhibited by the adversary; in the solitariness of the position in which the opponent was met: in the serenity of mind exhibited bythe conqueror; in the ministration of the celestial beings when the victory had been gained; and in the final triumph—there is some resemblance between the narration of the Scriptures and that of the Dharma. But no voice of comforting instruction proceeds from the bo-tree like that which is spoken by the apostle Paul "In all things it behoved him to be made like unto his brethren that he might be a merciful and faithful high priest in things pertaining to God, to make reconciliation for the sins of the people. For that he himself hath suffered, being tempted, he is able to succour them that are tempted."

BOOK III. THE MINISTRY

CHAPTER I.

THE COMMENCEMENT.

FIRST WORDS.

Nazareth, the despised, from its quietude and seclusion, was a place admirably adapted for forming the character of a Teacher whose doctrines and deliverances were to have little in common with any of the schools or sects then in existence. But Christ came not to teach alone, but to preach. He had to address the multitude "without," as well as to speak privately to the more favoured few, to whom it was "given to know the mystery of the kingdom of God." The light he was about to enkindle was not to be hid under a bushel, or to be of limited influence, but to blaze from the uplifted candlestick, that it might illumine the house of the world.

"Leaving Nazareth," he took up his abode in a central position, and dwelt in a city that lay between a-region the most intensely Jewish and a population the most decidedly Gentile. From this locality, "he went about all Galilee," thence his fame passed quickly onward, until it reached Jerusalem; but as the new prophet was of a province proverbially dark as the shadow of death, the report of his doings excited little attention on the part of the learned men of the metropolis. They took it for granted that no rival power they need fear could have its origin in the midst of a people so mixed in race, so ignorant of the law, and so turbulent in disposition.

The command that was to move the whole community was propounded in terms at once simple, authoritative and full of meaning: "Repent; for the kingdom of heaven is at hand." But these were regarded by the spiritual guides of the people as harmless words The old prophets had long ago inculcated repentance, but the effect they had produced was of small consequence. The Baptist had spoken of "the kingdom of heaven," but his influence was already on the wane. There was another element of a more marked character. It was said that he healed all manner of diseases, and cast out devils; but similar statements had been made of many men whose attempts to subvert the old polity had speedily come to nought. Meanwhile the leaven was beginning to work in the meal, the mustard-seep was passing from its littleness into a tree, and the kingdom was forming in the hearts of men. A mighty effect had been produced, before the rulers awoke to the consciousness, that a force was now existent, that would tend to the overthrow, of the entire fabric of the ecclesiastical system then in the ascendent.

THE SERMON ON THE MOUNT.

The unanointed peasant resident, as the Anointed of God, in a part of the land that was semi-heathen, was regarded at the beginning of his ministry with a feeling bordering upon disdain; but as the works he performed were such as none other man did, his character soon became more extensively known, and more reverently appreciated. Those who saw them were struck with astonishment, and told everywhere the story of what they had witnessed. The report was carried to many a homestead, and repeated with an earnestness of soul that sought to add to the importance of the announcement. "Where is he?" was the cry. Then Jesus, "seeing the multitude," who were gathering around him, and knowing that they were prepared to listen to his words, went up into a mountain in the same region, and placed himself in the position of one who was about to deliver a solemn address. The more thoughtful of those present wished to learn something further about "the kingdom" than they could learn from a mere echo of the words of John; and they were soon as much astonished at his doctrines as they had previously been at his deeds. They were so unlike all they had ever heard before that they were beside themselves, and concluded that the nation was on the eve of times that were to be glorious for Israel. The mystery of "the kingdom" is first explained. "Blessed are the poor in spirit; for theirs is the kingdom of heaven;" is the opening sentence of the address: referring again to the kingdom of which he had previously spoken. The effect of these first words of Christ was of varied character, as we have seen the flicker of the shadow when the cloud has passed rapidly over the corn-field waving on the hill side. The countenances of many assume an appearance that tells of sad disappointment and deep regret; whilst the frowning brow and angry scowl of others betoken a more indignant feeling. All these to be the princes and powers of the new kingdom; "the poor in spirit?" Is this the kind of monarchy that is to be established, and that has been ushered in by events that have made so many thousands wonder? But hear further. It may be that revelations are to be made that will be more in accordance with the general hope. "Blessed are they that mourn, for they shall be comforted," is the next utterance from the Teacher's lips; a twin sentence to the former; and in the like manner full of cheering encouragement to the humble and contrite in heart. Five other beatitudes follow in succession, all in perfect harmony with his first soft words, that have fallen gently and refreshingly upon the minds of those who are seeking a spiritual kingdom, in which shall reign unbroken peace; but acting like the flame lit up in the dry stubble-field upon those who would rather listen to a trumpet-blast mustering the hosts of Zion for the slaughter of the Philistines, the Gentile enemies of God. In the minds of some of the crowd there is agitation and perplexity, as if they know not whether to sanction or condemn; almost ready to express disapproval, but listening still, in the hope that something will be said that will be more soothing to their self-righteousness and more flattering to their pride. These are mostly of the Pharisees, to be easily distinguished by their broad phylacteries and the large and lettered borders of their robes. The doubt of the moment passes into lasting hatred and enmity, when the multitudes are taught rebel words against the men who regard themselves as the most enlightened exponents of the word of the Lord and the most exact in the practice of its precepts. "I say unto you, that except your righteousness shall exceed the righteousness of the Scribes and Pharisees ye shall in no case enter into the kingdom of heaven."

Glancing round at the expectant audience, the attention of Christ is attracted towards those whom he knows to be the sincere servants of God, and passing by the more pretentious of the groups who are before him, he comes at once to the timid, the afflicted, and the down-trodden; those who are most in need of consolation, and who are most overlooked in all systems that derive their authority from sources that are merely human,or that are invented for an earthly purpose. Sweet are the words of sympathy that as from an overflowing fountain of goodness, he pours into their grateful souls. Then seeing that there are many who are less prepared to enter into the kingdom, but who are sincerely jealous for the divine law, he next allays their rising doubts by assuring them that he had not come to destroy the law and the prophets, but to fulfil. Leaving all who are faithful with these thoughts, with a new life infused into their hearts, more joyous that the carol of the lark when it pours forth its soul that its music may mingle with the radiance of the summer's sunshine he assumes a graver aspect, and severely rebukes the subverters of the law, who have made it of none-effect, by their glosses and unauthorized additions. The principal subterfuges by which they have sought to make void the commands of God are unsparingly exposed; and in this revealing, the more specious of the sins of all communities are noted and condemned. The higher claims of the divine law are propounded, and an entire severance insisted upon from all affections that are incompatible with supreme love to God. But under the shadow of the wings of the Almighty the righteous may rest in entire confidence. No care that distresses need linger in the human breast; as men are under the constant regard of Him who feeds the ravens, and clothes the grass of the field with a glory greater than that of Solomon, and who will much more feed and clothe His own loving children, and supply all their wants.

Sakya Muni's First Sermon.

The circumstances attendant upon the delivering of the first sermon preached by Sákya Muni are minutely recorded; but with the usual want of historical truthfulness. There then surrounded him, not only "multitudes;" but we are told that all worlds poured forth their inhabitants that they might hear him, so that the congregation assembled was in numbers infinite. On the blowing of the shell of Indra "all became still as a waveless sea." The usual expression, when the Buddhists speak of the preaching of their sage, is, "he opened his lotus-like mouth." The evening upon which he thus preached is likened to a lovely female, with the stars as pearls around her neck, the fleecy clouds as her braided hair, and the expanse of the azure sky as her flowing robe; whilst her voice was like the hum of bees, her eyes were like expanded lilies, and the radiance of the lingering sunset as her golden crown. The poverty of the human beings who listened to the Muni was in contrast to the multitude who came from other worlds. His first audience consisted of the five ascetics who had lived with him for a time in the forest. When they saw him first after he had assumed the Buddhaship they resolved that they would pay him no respect as a teacher, though they were willing to honour him as a prince; but when they discovered the supreme dignity of his present character, they brought water to wash his feet, and treated him with the deference that was his due. These men were brahmans, of the highest, most honoured, and probably the most intelligent of the castes; so that it would appear that the first adherents of the Muni were men who were held in honour by the people, though he afterwards opened the privilege of discipleship equally to persons of all classes and conditions.

The discourse now delivered is called Dharma Chakka, the Circle, or the Wheel of the Truth. It contains the germ of the doctrines that are regarded as the most important in Buddhism, but no native work is known that professes to give a systematic account of his entire system. At the commencement he states that he has discovered a middle path, equally free from sensuous gratification and severe penance. "O priests, avoiding both these extremes, Buddha has perceived a middle path for the attainment of mental vision, true knowledge, subdued passion, the perception of the paths leading to the supreme good, the preparation necessary for attaining it, and the entrance to Nirvána." The first firm step in the march of discovery establishes the truth that "sorrow is connected with every mode of existence." The second step reveals the further conclusion, that this sorrow must continue so long as there is the existence of desire (the cleaving to sensuous objects.) This leads on to a third, that the extinction of desire must be attained by those who seek the destruction of sorrow; and then the assurance is given, that the extinction of desire can be attained by entering into "the path." Relative to this important concatenation he says, "O priests, possess the eye to perceive this previously undiscovered truth, the knowledge of its nature, the understanding of its cause, the wisdom to guide into the path of tranquillity, and the light to dispel darkness from it." There is no formal explanation of what is meant by the "path", but towards the conclusion he declares, "At that time (the night in which the truths now propounded were discovered) I know that I had acquired the most complete and irrefutable wisdom attainable in the universe. This wisdom and knowledge have sprung up within me. My mental deliverance is permanent. This is my last birth. I shall transmigrate no longer." After the first mention of nirvána there is no repetition of the mysterious word, but the meaning is to be gathered from the last sentence—it is the cessation of transmigratory existence.

The beatitudes of Christ might have been spoken on set purpose to disprove the conclusion of the Aryan Muni; so perfect is the contrast In the Dharma we have the confession, that by searching men cannot find unmixed happiness or perfect peace. Not only is vanity written upon all that is earthly—the petal of the expanded flower, the portal of the strong city, the centre circle of worldly pleasure, the scroll of the student, the treasure-house of the wealthy, and the sceptre of the monarch—inasmuch as all these must pass away. But the unrest of earth is found also in the highest state of bliss to which sentient existence can attain. The residence in heaven of the brightest and most glorious being among the celestial hosts is only for a limited period. There is no permanency in anything existent. The thought that all the pleasures Paradise can give are but transitory, and must be exchanged for some less privileged state, mars the sweetest of its enjoyments, and is as the evil eye ever overlooking the scene of joy, the sharp sword always hanging over the plenty of the banquet hall, the grim skeleton still standing near the wall of the mansion, by the side of youth and beauty, even when the trip of the dance is lightest and the music swells with its most maddening rush.

The confession of Muni is the deliberate conviction of an eastern philosopher, who has spent a series of years in the search of happiness and always in the mode most approved by the wise and good; and yet this is the cheerless terminus at which he arrives—to be free from sorrow there must be the suicide of existence. Live and you must necessarily be unhappy. Breathe; and you must necessarily be restless and in fear. The thought, thus presented, is the more depressing, as it is, to a great extent, an embodiment of the great mass of all pagan experience—not always expressed in terms so utterly hopeless; brightened, indeed, at times, by gleams of a better land; but seldom affording a resting-place for the soul in its hour of need, when the tempest gathers, and the streams rise and the howl of the wind is as the sigh of death The aim of the sage, we are free to confess, cannot have been to drive men to despair; and he reproduces the maxim, "Let us eat and drink for tomorrow we die" By thus presenting sentient existence—not only human life, but all existence—in its utmost helplessness, and declaring that there is no way to obtain release from its sorrows and sufferings but by following a prescribed course—moral and virtuous in the highest degree, so far as he understood the principles of morality and virtue—he sought to persuade men to avoid all that is evil and practice only that which is pure and good. We may consider that the motive of the Muni was right, whilst we deny entirely his conclusions, and equally question their power. We cannot conceive of men being deterred from sin by the thought that a holy life will lead him the more certainly to the nothingness of a nirvána.

The people were astonished at the Doctrine of Christ "for he taught them as one having authority and not as the Scribes

CHAPTER. II.

THE ASSERTION OF THE SUPREMACY.

"Be not ye called Rabbi, neither be called masters." Thus spake Jesus Christ, and he declared further. "He that is greatest among you shall be your servant."

No teacher of men has so thoroughly exposed the various phases of pride as Christ, or set forth with equal clearness, the beauty, power and heart-hallowing influence of humility. This was not done merely by dry precept or cold definition, but by the presentation of living example. Placing a little child in the midst of the twelve, who had disputed among themselves as to who was to be greatest in the kingdom of heaven he said, "Verily I say unto you, Except ye be converted and become as little children, ye shall not enter the kingdom of heaven. Matt. 18. 4. The Pharisees were rebuked by him because they loved the uppermost seats in the synagogue; his disciples were to choose the lowest room when bidden to a feast; and it was declared that "whosoever exalteth himself shall be abased, and he that humbleth himself shall be exalted." Luke. 14. 11.

And yet no one among the sons of men has asserted his own greatness more openly, more explicitly, or with greater constancy Though he refused to exercise the functions of the secular judge, and would pronounce no sentence affecting the interpretation of the national law, and rejected the offer of leadership made by the Jews in a moment of enthusiasm in all that related to the kingdom of God he assumed an authority that no human being had ever claimed before him, and that in any other teacher would have been the voice of blasphemy. In all his recorded sayings there is not one confession of inferiority, save in reference to the Father "I say unto you" were the words he used, when making known the divine will. The claim to receive equal honour with the Father was first asserted in a locality at a distance from the shadow of the sanhedrim, and might have seemed to be a daring act, done thus openly because there was no present fear of the consequences. But we see him, not long afterwards, in the heart of the holy city, in the very temple itself, with a scourge of small cords driving out the cattle-dealers and shrofs; saying also to them who sold doves, "Take these things hence; make not my Father's house an house of merchandise."

The stranger from Nazareth, who had come up with the other pilgrims to the feast of the Passover, though preceded by no herald, and attended by no lictor, was now acting as if he were held in honour by the people, though he afterwards opened the privilege of discipleship equally to persons of all classes and conditions.

The discourse now delivered is called Dharma Chakka, the Circle, or the Wheel of the Truth. It contains the germ of the doctrines that are regarded as the most important in Buddhism, but no native work is known that professes to give a systematic account of his entire system. At the commencement he states that he has discovered a middle path, equally free from sensuous gratification and severe penance "O priests, avoiding both these extremes, Buddha has perceived a middle path for the attainment of mental vision, true knowle[illegible] so secodued passion, the perception of the paths leading to of [illegible] supreme good, the preparation necessary for attaining it, and the entrance to nirvána." The first firm step in the march of discovery establishes the truth that "sorrow is connected with every mode of existence" The second step reveals the further conclusion, that this sorrow must continue so long as there is the existence of desire (the cleaving to sensuous objects.) This leads on to a third, that the extinction of desire must be attained by those who seek the destruction of sorrow; and then the assurance is given, that the extinction of desire can be attained by entering into "the path." Relative to this important concatenation he says, "I, O priests, possess the eye to perceive this previously undiscovered truth, the knowledge of its nature, the understanding of its cause, the wisdom to guide into the path of tranquillity, and the light to dispel darkness from it" There is no formal explanation of what is meant by the "path', but towards the conclusion he declares, "At that time (the night in which the truths now propounded were discovered) I know that I had acquired the most complete and irrefutable wisdom attainable in the universe. This wisdom and knowledge have sprung up within me. My mental deliverance is permanent. This is my last birth. I shall transmigrate no longer." After the first mention of nirvána there is no repetition of the mysterious word, but the meaning is to be gathered from the last sentence—it is the cessation of transmigratory existence.

The beatitudes of Christ might have been spoken on set purpose to disprove the conclusion of the Aryan Muni; so perfect is the contrast. In the Dharma we have the confession, that by searching men cannot find out unmixed happiness or perfect peace. Not only is vanity written upon all that is earthly—the petal of the expanded flower, the portal of the strong city, the entire circle of worldly pleasure, the scroll of the student, the treasure-house of the wealthy, and the sceptre of the monarch—inasmuch as all these must pass away. But the unrest of earth is found also in the highest state of bliss to which sentient existence can attain. There is no permanency in anything existent. The residence in heaven of the brightest and most glorious being among the celestial hosts is only for a limited period. The thought that all the pleasures Paradise can give are but transitory, and must be exchanged for some less privileged state, mars the sweetest of its enjoyments, and is as the evil eye ever overlooking the scene of joy, the sharp sword always hanging over the plenty of the banquet hall, the grim skeleton still standing near the wall of the mansion, by the side of youth and beauty, even when the trip of the dance is lightest and the music swells with its most maddening rush.

The confession of Muni is the deliberate conviction of a calm philosopher, who has spent a series of years in the search of happiness and always in the mode most approved by the wise and good; and yet this is the cheerless terminus at which he arrives--to be free from sorrow there must be the suicide for existence. Breathe; and you must necessarily be restless and in fear. Live and you must necessarily be unhappy. The thought, thus presented, is the more depressing, as it is, to a great extent, an embodiment of the great mass of all pagan experience—not always expressed in terms so utterly hopeless; brightened, indeed, at times, by gleams of a better land; but seldom affording a resting-place for the soul in its hour of need, when the tempest gathers, and the streams rise and the howl of the wind is as the sough of death. The aim of the sage, we are free to confess, cannot have been to drive men to despair; and he repudiates the maxim, "Let us eat and drink for tomorrow we die." By thus presenting sentient existence—not only human life, but all existence—in its utmost helplessness, and declaring that there is no way to obtain release from its sorrows and sufferings but by following a prescribed course—moral and virtuous in the highest degree, so far as he understood the principles of morality and virtue—he sought to persuade men to avoid all that is evil and practice only that which is pure and good. We may consider that the motive of the Muni was right, whilst we deny entirely his conclusions, and equally question their power. We cannot conceive of men being deterred from sin by the thought that a holy life will lead him the more certainly to the nothingness of a nirvána.

The people were astonished at the doctrine of Christ, "for he taught them as one having authority and not as the scribes."

CHAPTER II.

THE ASSERTION OF THE SUPREMACY.

"Be not ye called Rabbi, neither be called masters" Thus spake Jesus Christ, and he declared further, "He that is greatest among you shall be your servant."

No teacher of men has so thoroughly expressed the various phases of pride as Christ, or set forth with equal clearness, the beauty, power and heart-hallowing influence of humility. This was not done merely by dry precept or cold definition, but by the presentation of living example. Placing a little child in the midst of the twelve, who had disputed among themselves as to who was to be greatest in the kingdom of heaven he said, "Verily I say unto you, Except ye be converted and become as little children, ye shall not enter the kingdom of heaven." Matt 11. 4. The Pharisees were rebuked by him because they loved the uppermost seats in the synagogue; his disciples were to choose the lowest room when bidden to a feast; and it was declared that "whosoever exalteth himself shall be abased, and he that humbleth himself shall be exalted." Luke 14. 11.

And yet no one among the sons of men has asserted his own greatness more openly, more explicitly, or with greater constancy. Though he refused to exercise the functions of the secular judge, and would pronounce no sentence affecting the interpretation of the national law, and rejected the offer of leadership made by the Jews in a moment of enthusiasm, in all that related to the kingdom of God he assumed an authority that no human being had ever claimed before him, and that in any other teacher would have been the voice of blasphemy. In all his recorded sayings there is not one confession of inferiority, save in reference to the Father. "I say unto you" were the words he used, when making known the divine will. The claim to receive equal honour with the Father was first asserted in a locality at a distance from the shadow of the sanhedrim, and might have seemed to be a daring act, done thus openly because there was no present fear of the consequences. But we see him, not long afterwards, in the heart of the holy city, in the very temple itself, with a scourge of small cords driving out the cattle-dealers and shrofs; saying also to them who sold doves, "Take these things hence; make not my Father's house an house of merchandise."

The stranger from Nazareth, who had come up with the other pilgrims to the feast of the Passover, though preceded by no herald, and attended by no lictor, was now acting as if he were already "king in Jeshurun; and was enunciating utterances that involved a claim to the profession of the very throne of Jehovah. The kingdom was spoken of still, but henceforth there was more frequent reference to the Father: yet ever avoiding the phrase, "Our Father," as if he alone inherited the higher Sonship, and possessed it in some sense essentially different to the adoption that is the common privilege of the children of God. To one of his earliest disciples he said, "Hereafter ye shall see heaven open, and the angels of God ascending and descending upon the Son of man." John i. 51 By the "Son of man" we are made to understand that he himself is intended, as he asks at another time, "Whom do men say that I, the Son of man, am?" Matt. xvi. 13. There are subsequently words of strongest power, spoken in relation to his character by himself; and not by some ardent disciple, who might have been mistaken in the conclusion he formed respecting his mysterious Master. "Neither knoweth any man the Father, save the Son." Matt. xi. 27. "My Father worketh hitherto, and I work." John v. 17. "All men should honour the Son even as they honour the Father." v. 23. "As the Father raiseth up the dead, and quickeneth them, even so the Son quickeneth whom he will." v. 21. "All things that the Father hath are mine." xvi. 15. "He that hath seen me hath seen the Father." xiv. 9 "I and my Father are one." x. 30. At the utterance of the last expression, "the Jews took up stones again to stone him:" they knew its import.

The claim to equality with God, thus plainly asserted, was inferentially reiterated in the power he assumed over the Church of the future, and in the promises and commands he gave to its pastor and people. He has the bread of life, and proclaims that whoever came to him should never hunger, and that whoever believed on him should never thirst. John v. 36. He gave to Peter the keys of the kingdom of heaven. Matt. xvi. 19. He said, "And I, if I be lifted up, will draw all men after me." John xii. 37. As the Father had sent him, so he sent his disciples. As Lord of the Sabbath, he defined the requirements of the sacred day. Mark ii. 28. With the simple preface, "I will" or, "I say," he established the law,

Matt. v. 28, forgave sins, Mark ii. 9. He asserted the power to lay down his own life, and to take it up again; and made known that whosoever kept his sayings should not see death, that the dead would hear his voice, and at tke hearing thereof would rise from their graves and live; he said that he would come in the clouds of heaven, in the glory of the Father and of the holy angels; and that before him would be gathered all nations, when he would place some on his right hand, assigning to these everlasting blessedness, and some on his left hand, to whom he would appoint the doom of everlasting woe. After his resurrection he breathed on them and said unto them, "Whose soever sins ye remit, they are remited unto them; and whose soever sins ye retain they are retained." John xx. 21. And just before his departure from earth when the everlasting door were about to be uplifted for the entrance of the King of Glory upon the royal state he had possessed before the world was, he said to the apostles, "Go ye, therefore and teach all nations, baptizing them in the name of the Father, and of the Son, and of the Holy Ghost: teaching them to observe all things whatsoever I have commanded you: and, lo, I am with you always, even unto the end of the world."

After listening to these sayings of Christ, we are placed in this position, that we must either say with Peter, "Thou art the Christ, the Son of the living God;" or we must say with the unbelieving Jews, "Nay, but he deceiveth the people." But we accept the conclusion of Nicodemus, "Rabbi, we know that thou art a teacher come from God, for no man can do the miracles that thou doest, except God be with him." It follows, as a necessary corollary, that we are called upon to present him the homage of the whole heart, and place our entire trust in his Gospel, as containing "the words of eternal life."

In the earlier chapters of revelation, there is no assertion of the supremacy of God, nor any definition of the divine attributes. We see God first in the act of creation: and as the light bursts forth upon the world at his command, and the waters separate from the dry land, and the low grass creeps over the far-extending lea, and the cereals yield the seed that is to produce the golden harvest, and the trees are laden with the rich fruits that are presently to be the food of man; and the sun, moon, and stars appear; and the fish glide rapidly through the waters, the insect hums in the air, the bird utters its first notes of sweet song, and the beast paws the ground in majesty; and the man and woman, gifted with all that is lovely or graceful, assume the universal sovereignty; we learn therefrom more about the grandeur of the Godhead than could have been taught by many volumes filled with comment and exposition. We are thus prepared for the proclaiming of the divine law, and are ready at once to acknowledge its authority and the justice of its demands upon the obedience of the human race. Somewhat after the same manner, the dignity of Jesus Christ, the Son of God, who rescued the moral world from chaos, and is its second Creator, was first revealed to the men of Israel. After an announcement relative to the coming kingdom, he plainly intimated his right to the monarchy of the new realm by cleansing the leper, imparting sight to the blind, and casting out devils; and then there was the authoritative annunciation of the doctrines that were to be taught and the laws that were to be enacted when the new polity was established. But if Christ had spoken from the throne of God, surrounded by lightnings vivid as those that flashed from the crests of Sinai, and in tones terrible as its thunders, he could not have asserted his claim to be acknowledged by all nations as their Master and Lord, in terms more commanding or comprehensive than are heard in the sayings that are recorded as proceeding from his lips.

The wisdom ascribed to Sákya Muni, and by virtue of which he claimed the supreme Buddhaship was said to be self-emanated. He was called the Tathágata, meaning that he had come in the same way as the previous Buddhas. But each Buddha teaches the same doctrines; not because they have been taught by his predecessors, but because they are immutable and eternal truths We may smile at the absurdity of the legend, that immediately after his birth he proceeded seven steps, and after looking in every direction exclaimed as with the voice of a fearless lion, "I am the most exalted being in the world, the chief and the most excellent." But in the discourses he is said to have delivered after he became Buddha, there is assertion, continually repeated, of the same arrogant character. He declared that there was no being in the whole universe who was entitled to receive from him salutation or reverence, or before whom he ought to stand up, or whom he ought to invite to be seated in his presence· nay, that if he condescended thus to act, and the invitation were accepted, the head of the person so presuming would undoubtedly fall from his body. The reason why this deference should be paid to him is found towards the end of the first discourse on the Parájeká, in addressing a brahmin who had come to converse with him, and who expostulated with him on the marks of respect he claimed, as "not consistent with propriety." The extract * we make from this discourse is a fair specimen of the mode of thought presented in the Dharma and gives as clear an in-sight into its general principles as any example within our reach, and in the same compass.

"Bramin, if eight, ten, or twelve eggs are placed under a hen and carefully batched, what appellation is given to the bird who with his foot, his spur, his head, or his beak, first breaks his egg, and is perfectly formed?" "Such an one, venerable Goutama, should be called 'The Chief' ජෙට්ඨො he is the first born." "Even so, Bramin, having broken the shell of ignorance by which, enveloped in darkness, all beings were encompassed, I stood alone in the Universe, in the full ascertainment of unerring and all-perfect knowledge. I, Bramin, am the first born, the Chief of the World. Bramin, I was persevering and diligent, thoughtful and intelligent, tranquil in body and mind, with a pure heart and with singleness of purpose. Being, Bramin, free from sensuality and criminal propensities, I enjoyed the pleasures of the first Jhána (or course of profound meditation) produced by retirement spent in examination and investigation.

"Investigation and research being terminated, with internal serenity and a mind concentrated in itself, I enjoyed the pleasure of the Second Jhána, produced by the tranquillity which is undisturbed by enquiry or investigation.

"Free from the disturbances of pleasure, contented, thoughtful and wise, and possessed of health of body, I experienced the happiness of the third Jhána, called by holy sages the happy state of thoughtful contentment.

"Free from the emotions of joy or sorrow, previous exultation and depression being annihilated, I lived with a contented mind, unmoved either by pleasure or pain, and being perfectly holy, attained to the fourth Jhána.

"Being thus mentally tranquil, pure and holy, free from passion or pollution, serene, and competent to the effort, I addressed my mind to the recollection of former stages of existence. I remembered these states of previous being from one birth up to those experienced during many revolutions of kalpas, and recalled to mind the place where I resided, the name I bore, my race and family, my circumstances, personal appearance, enjoyments and sufferings, and the duration of

---

* Vide Essay on Buddhism, read by the Rev. D. J. Gogerly, before the Ceylon Branch of the Royal Asiatic Society, part 1 page 6. May. 1st, 1845.

life, at the conclusion of which I ceased to live there and was born in another place, until I was born in this world. Thus I recalled to mind former states of existence, with their circumstances and causes. Thus Bramin, during the first watch of the night, ignorance passed away and knowledge was obtained; darkness was dispersed and the light shone forth; and by my persevering and holy exertion, like the first hatched chicken, I first chipped the shell of ignorance.

"Being thus mentally tranquil, pure and holy, free from the pollution of the passions, serene and competent to the effort, I addressed myself to the consideration of the birth and death of intelligent beings, and with a clear and godlike vision, transcending that of men, I looked upon beings, dying and being born, whether noble or base, beautiful or deformed, happy or sorrowful, according to the desert of their previous conduct. I saw some whose conduct was evil in thought word and deed, revilers of holy men, holders of false doctrines and attached to the observances of a false religion; these, upon the dissolution of the body after death, were produced in hell, increasing in misery, wretchedness and torments.

"I saw some who were virtuous in thought word and deed, who reverenced holy men, were of a pure faith, and attached to the observances of the true religion; these upon the dissolution of the body, after death, were born in heaven endued with felicity. Thus Bramin, during the second watch of the night, the second part of ignorance passed away and knowledge was obtained; darkness was dispersed and the light shone forth; and by my persevering and holy exertion, like the first hatched chicken, I again chipped the shell of ignorance.

"Being thus mentally tranquil, pure and holy, free from the pollution of the passions, serene and competent to the effort, I turned my attention to that wisdom by which desire can be extinguished: and clearly discerned, according to its real nature, this is sorrow; this is the source of sorrow; this is the cessation of sorrow; this is the path by which cessation from sorrow may be obtained. These are the desires: these are the causes of their production. This is the extinction of of desire. This is the path leading to the cessation of desire. Having understood and perceived these truths, my mind became free from sensual desires, free from the desire of continual existence, and free from ignorance; I became conscious that I possessed this freedom, and certainly knew that my transmigrations were terminated, my course of virtues completed, my needful work accomplished, and that nothing more remained to be done.

"Thus Bramin, during the third watch of the night, the third part of ignorance passed away and knowledge was obtained; the darkness was dispersed and the light shone forth; and by my persevering and holy exertion, like the first hatched chicken I broke the shell of ignorance."

From this extract we learn that Sákya Muni founded his claim to supremacy upon being perfect in purity, entirely free from the influence of desire whether in reference to bodily and mental sensation or the continuance of transmigratory existence, and upon his being perfect in knowledge, of whatever kind. Acknowledging no teacher, no inspiration from a higher source, he declares himself to be the fountain of knowledge for all existing beings, whatever may be their dignity. But we can place no confidence in himself, or in the system that bears his name, as his life is a myth, his teaching a mass of error, his code of morals imperfect, and his religion founded on principles that have no substantiality.

CHAPTER III.

THE EVIDENCE IN PROOF OF THE SUPREMACY.

No prophet has ever been divinely commissioned to make a new announcement, enforce a new command, institute a new ceremony, or teach a new doctrine, who has not been enabled to fortify his declaration, "thus saith the Lord," by the power to stay, or modify, or intensify some process in the usual economy of the world, that no man could accomplish unless through the power of God. Nearly all pretenders to inspiration have claimed the possession of this order of witness; and if it was not in something that could be made manifest to others, its presence was nevertheless asserted, as in the memorable instance of Mahomet, who wrought "no miracle," as the phenomenon is usually defined; but by affirming that the Angel Gabriel spoke to him the words of Allah, he would have it to be understood that this voice superseded all outward and visible signs and wonders, and rendered them unnecessary for the confirmation of his mission. So all who are convinced of the existence of God, and that we have proofs of the divine interest and interference in the governance of the world, the probability of the occurrence of what are called miracles will be apparent. Otherwise, we seek to reduce God to a mere machine, moving in one undeviating course, like the stellar system in its regularity. Or, in other words, we give to God less freedom than is possessed by the most insignificant creature that has a will.

In mercy to man, God has appointed certain sequences that we call the laws of nature, which under ordinary circumstances work according to one rule, without variableness. But in equal mercy, for the promotion of his own glory or the greater benefit to mankind, there are occasions when this law is superseded by another law, for the time of greater importance. We give to this working the name of law, on the same principle that we say the sun rises; because the sequence appears like a law to us, and the miracle an exception; but in the mind of God the exception is as much a part of the law as the usual sequence. Given the fact that the divine interference is ever occurrent in human affairs, there will be little difficulty in conceding that evidences of its existence will be seen the most clearly in matters that affect the higher interests of mankind, those connected with religion.

A miracle is only an extension of the law of exceptions; of which we have so many similar instances in the events that take place in the world around us.

The mission of the ancient prophets was to individuals, or at the most to separated nations, so that it was commonly local or temporary in its influence. That of Christ was to all generations and people who should afterwards exist, even to the end of the world We are not prepared for a new order of miracles, to give evidence that it was of God, as this would have been a deviation tending to excite doubt; but we expect to see a manifestation of the same class of events, in greater frequency of occurence and with stronger signs of beneficence of character; and from his divinity we infer that they will be accompanied by more decided proofs of self-emanation in their origin, that they will be of wider range and present a greater grandeur of purpose. All these desiderata concentrate in the miracles of Christ.

1. Of the frequency of their occurrence, it may be enough to say, that from the beginning of miracles at Cana of Galilee, when the water was turned into wine, to the healing of the ear of the servant Malchus in the garden of Gethsemane, there is scarcely a page in the narration of the evangelists on which some mighty work is not recorded In many cases, one record includes many separate acts, as when it is said that "he healed them all"—the sick, the diseased, the lunatic, and those possessed by devils,—and when he fed the multitude with a few barley loaves and two small fishes; and the apostle John tells us that there "are also many other things which Jesus did" that are not written.

2. With the exception of the entrance of the devils into the herd of swine and the withering of the fig-tree, all the miracles of Christ were at once seen to be of a merciful character. In the former instance, if the swineherds were Gentiles, they were presenting a dangerous temptation to the Jews to break the law, by preparing hog's flesh for the market; and if they were Jews, they were following an unlawful occupation; and the permission to enter into the swine was given at the request of the devils themselves, for some reason we may not be able fully to comprehend In the other instance, the non-sentient fig-tree was rendered unfruitful "for ever," that the generation of living Jews might learn an instructive lesson, and turn from

their sins, lest a greater condemnation should befall them. We are not necessitated to homologate the words of Peter, and say that it was "cursed," as if the withering was an unholy act of sudden indignation.

There is a delicacy of kindness and good-will about many of the miracles of Christ that immeasurably highten their beauty, as the mosaic of the story is arranged on the sacred page. By his first miracle, he sanctified the rejoicing at the wedding feast in celebration of all virtuous nuptials; his compassion was extended to the leper, whose touch was regarded as pollution; the "grievously tormented," for whom his aid was sought by the centurion, was only a servant, but he did not upon that account refuse to listen to the request; the great multitude of fishes was enclosed in the net which brake, that they who were now called to be "fishers of men" might receive courage to trust in One who had no earthly possession, but for whom they were about to leave "all;" the impotant man, labouring under the infirmity of thirty and eighty years, was made whole, because he saw that he had been now a long time in that case; it was to hush the fears of his disciples when there was a great tempest, that he stilled the winds and the sea, and said to them, "Peace, be still;" the sick of the palsy, borne of four, received the forgiveness of his sins, as well as the power to walk; the voice of the despised woman was as powerful to gain his sympathy as that of the lordly man; in the gift of sight to the blind there was imparted the power savingly to believe; he fed the thousands in the wilderness by the multiplying of a few loaves and fishes, lest on their return home they should faint in the way; he cast out the devil at the foot of the mount of transfiguration, with expressions of deep sorrow for the unbelief of his disciples; he healed the blind men who were sitting by the way-side because he had compassion on them; the voice that cried out at the grave near Bethany, "Lazarus, come forth," had a few moments previously been broken by the groan of anguish, which told how tenderly he loved the dead; when in the garden that was saturated with his own blood, he healed the servant of the high priest, though that servant had accompanied the men who came to seize him as a wrong-doer. Each of these events was as much a miracle of beneficence as of power; of mercy as of might.

3. In no instance was there the seeking of foreign aid; nor was there any acknowledgment by which trust in an influence or potentiality not inherent in himself could be infered. Before the mourners at Bethany he thanked the Father, "because of the people which stood by," and he asked the Father to

glorify his own name; but we have no instance in which he prayed to the Father to assist him in the working of a miracle. In the power he exerted over the natural world there was the same great exercise of conscious prerogative that was evinced in relation to the divine law and its requirements. The effect was sometimes produced by a touch from his own hand; sometimes by the contact of others with his person, or even his raiment; but more usually by a simple utterance. "He spake and it was done." Though faith was declared as being so necessary upon the part of his disciples, it is never represented as being exercised by Christ. The miracle was never the consequence of spell, or incantation, or exorcism. Peter, at the gate called Beautiful, when the lame man was restored, said unto the people, "Ye men of Israel, why marvel ye at this? or why look ye so earnestly on us, as though by our own power we had made this man to walk?" but when the apostles worshipped Christ after the storm, because the winds and the waves obeyed him, he did not rebuke them, or refuse to receive their homage.

4. The power exercised by Christ was of the most extended and diversified character. The fish caught in the net when it was let down at his "command," and the stater brought in the mouth of the fish for the payment of tribute, the sap arrested in the blighted fig-tree, gave evidence to his rule over the animal, vegetable, and mineral kingdoms. The instant slumbering of the winds that had rushed down in fury from the mountains a moment before, and the calm upon the sea that at once succeeded the agitation of the storm, gave witness that when he spake the elements of air and water alike obeyed his voice. Each member of the body, whether it were the eye, the ear, the tongue, the hand, or the foot, though previously inert or motionless, stirred into health and use at his bidding. Each disease, whether from fever, leprosy, or paralysis, fled at his rebuke. The devils departed from the souls they had possessed at what time, or in what manner, he decreed. In the chamber of death, by the uplifted bier, at the grave itself, it was seen, in a manner that none could gainsay that his authority extended to other worlds, and that he had only to issue his decree, and sheol would give up its dead.

5. Jesus Christ ever referred to his own resurrection as the greatest and most convincing proof the Jews would receive that he spake the word of truth. This was the final link in the chain of testimony completing the evidence that he had "come from God." While he was yet alive, he repeatedly

declared that in three days after his death he would rise again. The chief priests were aware of the prediction, and of the time to which its fulfilment was limited. We may be sure that all possible care would be taken to prevent it. But on the morning of the third day it was announced that the sepulchre was empty ; the body was not there. The soldiers on guard did not see him rise, as our painters represent. It was whilst the seal of the sanhedrim was yet unbroken, and the watch were yet unconscious that their vigilance had been in vain, that he arose; and it was on the appearance of an angel that the soldiers shook with fear, and "became as dead men." The death of Christ had been openly declared, after official inquest. Had the body not been in the possession of his enemies, it might have been said that the foretelling was invented to prepare the minds of the people for the story told by the disciples. But they had the body in their own keeping. Thus, they were themselves the principal witnesses of the truth of the event they had hoped to hinder. They said that whilst the guard slept the body was stolen by the disciples. If the soldiers were asleep, we ask the careless custodes how they knew in what manner, or by whom the theft was accomplished ; and if what they said was true, we ask, why did not the priests insist on the guard being put to death, according to usage, for a breach of military discipline, when they saw that their neglect would produce the most disastrous issue that could possibly have happened to their polity. The real thought of these wretched men was revealed, when they confessed to fear lest the consequences of his death might be brought upon them, and in the great day that was to overtake the then existing generation the appalling spectre of "this man's blood" must have produced overwhelming terror. The populace possibly knew nothing about the guard, as it is evident that the women did not; and from their stand-point it was not so unlikely a conclusion that the body had been furtively taken away. But if the disciples were connected with the alleged theft, we are very certain that Peter would have been foremost in the larceny : and yet this man, a few days afterwards, and in the same place, with the consciousness that if he would only confess to having joined in a deceptive deed, untold wealth was at his command, fearlessly proclaimed to the house of Israel that he whom they had crucified was "both Lord and Christ," nor could the thong of the scourger or the gaoler's gyves deter him from its repetition.

We are now prepared to acknowledge the full force and absolute conclusiveness of the words of Christ. "I have greater witness than that of John, for the works that the Father hath given me to finish, the same works that I do, bear witness of me, that the Father hath sent me." From the nature of these works, they could not be, as the ancient heathen said and as the Jews now say, by the power of magic; and from their design they could not be, as his contemporaries said, by the power of the devil; and we are shut up to the conviction that they were wrought, as he himself says, "by the finger of God."

The miraculous powers attributed to Sákya Muni are far beyond the comprehension of the western mind; and their intended purpose is defeated by their exaggerated character, which is hyperbolical, beyond all precedent. The importance of having accredited witnesses to the validity of his claim to the Buddhaship was acknowledged by himself, at so early a period as his contest with Mara. But as events that we should regard as supernatural were then of every day occurence, and were acknowledged to be within the power of unbelievers as well as his own disciples, he professed not to appeal to miracles as an evidence that his teachings were true, affecting to despise them in comparison with the power of the Dharma itself to produce conviction; and instancing the case of a fire-worshipper, who had witnessed great numbers of miracles unmoved, but was converted to the faith by listening to one single discourse of the Muni.

According to the commonly-received legends, the sage was accompanied by miracles through the whole of his existence. On his first appearance among men the thirty-two wonders that were seen, including the temporary cessation of the pains and penalties of hell, extended to ten thousand worlds. We have already recorded the words he uttered immediately after his birth. When five months old, he sat in the air, without any visible support, at a ploughing festival. From the time of his reception of the Buddhaship, there was a halo of glory encircling his head, that extended to a distance of six cubits. It is represented in the image made of him as of the same shape as the cloven tongues of fire, figured by our painters as resting upon the apostles on the day of Pentecost. All obstructions removed from his pathway of their own accord; muddy places became dry; depressions were filled up and elevations levelled; all pains ceased at his approach, and at every step a lotus flower sprung up from the ground. He could walk in a space not larger than a mustard-seed, and could mount to the top of the large mountain in the centre of the world in three steps; yet he did not increase in size, or the mountain become less. When he delivered a discourse, each being in the extended circle around him supposed that his eyes were fixed upon himself. Though he spoke in the language of Màgadha, each listener thought he was addressed in his own language; and even birds and animals could so far understand him, as to receive merit from his instruction.

In that which is intended for history, the incidents recorded of the life are of a similar description. When he threw towards the heavens the hair he cut off on becoming a mendicant, it remained suspended in the sky; and the alms-bowl he was afterwards to use was brought to him by the four divine guardians of heaven. When the disciples of the fire-worshipper, Uruwela, were attempting to cleave wood for an offering, the Muni made the logs appear as if they were of pitch or lead so that they could not be cloven, and the arms of some, when uplifted, remained fixed in the air. The wood would not kindle until Buddha gave permission, and then the fire could not be extinguished without his interference. During one of his visits to the Nigrodha grove he caused a fire to proceed from his person; but though it extended to many worlds. it did not burn even a cobweb; and at the same place, he caused an image of himself to appear in the sky, and the two Buddhas held a conversation with each other. He thrice visited Ceylon, going to it through the air; at the third visit leaving an impression of his foot; which was to be a seal that Lanka was taken under his protection, and that his religion would there flourish. The city of Wisata being afflicted at one and the same time by pestilence, famine, and sprites, by whom the death of multitudes was caused, a request was made to the Muni that he would visit the place and free the people from the calamities by which they were afflicted. On entering the city he commanded his attendant, Ananda, to take his alms-bowl, and sprinkle water from it, as he went along. At once the sick were restored to health, and the sprites fled to some other place. In the city of Sewat, after eating a mangoe fruit, he directed his attendants to set it in the ground, and to throw on it the water with which he had rinsed his mouth; when, in a moment, the earth clove, a sprout appeared, and a tree arose, which overspread the city. But on the same occasion the monk Mugalan declared that he could roll up the earth like a mat, and cover it with his finger, and that he could turn the world upside down, as if it were a water-jug.

Three several times Buddha's life was sought; by means of an intoxicated elephant, a company of archers, and a machine that could hurl rocks; but the elephant, on seeing him, instantly became sober; the archers on listening to him, felt so much affection for him that they at once became his friends; and the rock on approaching his person, having become broken into two pieces, only a small fragment struck his foot, causing a slight wound. On seeing these things, his enemies were convinced that it was not possible to do him any serious injury, and they desisted from any further attempt against him.

One of the most notable exhibitions of the power and glory of the Muni was in a visit he paid to the heaven of Indra, for the purpose of preaching the Dharma to its inhabitants. Eighty-three days were occupied in the service, during which he recited the whole of the Abhidharma Pitaka. The faithful awaited his return to earth in anxious expectation. Seven days after the conclusion of the discourse, Indra caused a ladder of glory to extend from heaven to earth, on each side of which was another ladder, one of gold, by which the celestial choristers descended, and the other of silver, on which the gods appeared, bearing canopies, and banners To the people who saw these wonders, the ladders seemed like so many rainbows. Thus attended, Buddha came down from the abode of the déwas, surrounded by all the splendour with which heaven could grace his descent. The central ladder disappeared under the earth.

We have here presented only a few specimens of the numerous tales that appear in the sacred books of the Buddhists, invented to add to the reverence with which his followers are taught to regard their sage; but in reality throwing doubt and denial upon the whole series of narratives, by the impossibility of their occurrence. By history and science they are equally disproved. There could not have been men flying through the air in the time of the prophet Daniel, without some record of the event in western lore; and no power ever exercised among men could put a mountain into the shell of a mustard seed.

There are a few, and but a few, coincidences between the miracles ascribed to Buddha and those recorded of Christ. The miracles of the Muni were all intended to confer some benefit upon those who witnessed them or in whose behalf they were performed. Even when he declared that in seven days his unbelieving father-in-law would go down to hell, and the earth opened and sent forth flames, the punishment was not caused by the prediction, but was the consequence of his own misdeeds. Buddha never wrought a miracle for the supply of his own wants, and after the performance of one he would never allow his monks to seek alms in the same place, as he said that this would be like the manner of mountebanks and jugglers, who exhibit their skill, and then make a collection from the crowd. But the witnesses to the works performed by the Muni fail in the testimony they present. We might as soon believe the stories we are told of Sinbad the sailor, and of the valiant giant-slayer of Cornwall, as the tales that are related of Sàkya Muni and his disciples; whilst the miracles of Christ were many of them seen by the writers from whom we receive the account of them, and were not denied by the opponents of the Gospel, though they ascribed them to a wrong source. They are simple, possible and credible; above reason, but not contradicting it; suited to the circumstances under which they took place; consistent with the character of God; instructive in the lessons they teach; and ever accompanied by high and holy purpose.

CHAPTER IV.

THE VOICE OF THE TEACHER.

We should conclude, from a priori reasoning, if we were told that a being had come down from heaven, and appeared among men, that he would have little about him that was purely human, and that the unearthliness of his origin would be apparent even to the less discriminating observer, and detected in all his words and ways; and if such a being were a creature of the imagination alone, we should still conclude, that in order to make the high character given to him appear natural, he would be represented as living in a sphere far away from the influences that affect ordinary mortals. But in the accounts we possess of Jesus Christ, we have the reverse of these inductions. He stands before us, a thorough man in all things that are "without sin;" the most human of human beings. The russet of home, warm in its texture, and of spotless purity is the drapery with which the Saviour is invested in the evangelical portraiture of the Son of man. The sympathies of the heart are seen in unbroken outflow. He is a man of sorrows, and touched with the feeling of man's infirmities. He is as familiar with the sighs of earth as with the songs of heaven; and the quiet scenes of domestic life rise up before his mind as readily as the music and majesty of the palace of God.

The similitudes and illustrations used by Christ are of a like homely order. When he would tell of "Solomon in all his glory," he does not go to the angel of bliss or the morning stars, but to the lily of the field; probably some plant that grew wild near the shore of the sea of Galilee, the form of which was known to all. If a bird is required to express the care of God for man, he does not take us to the eagle, sailing majestically in the blue ether far away from the shaft of the most skilful archer, but to the sparrow, with no elevation in its flight, no attractiveness in the colour of its plumage, and no melody in its voice; as he knew that it accompanies man in all his wanderings, and nestles under the eaves of his dwelling in all climes; so that it is called in Chinese "the home bird," and seems almost conscious of its divine commission, as it everywhere cheers man by its twitter and chirp.

When the people were unwilling to receive what he taught them as to the real nature of "the kingdom," Christ adopted less frequently the mode of instruction in fragment or outline, as seen in the salt of the household, the oven with its kindling of grass, the city on the hill, and the corrupt tree bringing forth evil fruit, and used the parable in its perfect pictorial form, sometimes without comment or exegesis. This attracted the attention of the twelve, who said to him, "Why speakest thou unto them in parables?" The reply was in union with a great law in the moral government of God; that 'whosoever hath, to him shall be given, and he shall have more abundance; but whosoever hath not, from him shall be taken away even that he hath." By the interest of the story the attention of the multitude was secured. It was then within their own power to profit by the word or reject its guidance. Nothing was said on set purpose to mystify the Saviour's meaning. The living seed is provided, and it remains with the husbandman to let it abide as it falls, unfruitful until its vitality is gone, or to harrow it into the earth of the mind, and by culture make it yield a rich harvest. The light is presented before the eye; but if they who see it, wander away from its influence into the darkness, their gloom of soul becomes deeper thereby; whilst, if they are willing to be guided by it, and follow in the way that it indicates as the path of safety, it will lead them onward to the unclouded sunshine of the perfect day.

With two exceptions, the scene of all the parables in the Gospel is laid in some familiar portion of the Jewish house or village, or in some well-known locality. Much might be witnessed without stirring away from the shelter of the good man's own dwelling, or the shadow of the tree near which his children played his evening meal was taken in the soft twilight, and his neighbours sat when they came to gossip. Inside the house, we have the lighted candle, the bushel, the salt, the leaven, the loaves of bread, the yoke, the new and old bottles, the patches of cloth, and the lost piece of silver. All these become vocal at the call of Christ, and speak words pregnant with saving knowledge. The children of the bride chamber, the labourers waiting to be hired; the cloud, the sound of the wind, and the red sky; the tares, the basket of fish, and the spreading fig-tree; the shepherd and his flock, the unfaithful steward and his ten thousand talents, and the rich man with his overflowing barns; are instances in which a single fact may represent a multitude of others, of a similar character, that appear in the instructions given by Christ to those who thronged around him that they might listen to his attractive words. The two exceptions to which we have referred relate to the seven more wicked spirits and to the rich man tormented in hell; but the truths they taught could not have been conveyed by means of earthly imagery alone; and yet they were too important to remain without announcement.

In the synagogue and the temple the doctrines of the Gospel were revealed to the people, but they were most commonly given, especially in the early part of his ministry, in the places where the neglected multitudes could the most readily be gathered together He taught in the house, and the street, on the slope of the hill ; by the way-side and the sea-shore ; and the lay character of the surrounding scenery must in many instances have been in unison with the simplicity of the style he adopted, so unlike what would have been heard if one of their own doctors had been the prolocutor. It was as unlike that of any other teacher, as his works were unlike those of any other prophet. There was a nearer creeping to man's heart of sorrow ; a more reverent listening to its murmur and mourning, as seen when the bent ear of affection seeks most anxiously to catch the scarcely audible expression of its wants. It seems so natural to be told of the beloved disciple—that he learned upon Jesus' bosom. We learn further, that "the common people heard him gladly." He spoke to them in their own mothers' talk ; every word a household word ; and subjects that when handled in the schools were deep mysteries, he explained in such manner that the commonest understanding could comprehend them. Even the uninstructed did not weary with listening to him. He had on more than one occasion to send his audience away; for in the wilderness thousands were still waiting to hear more, though they had been there three days, and had nothing to eat.

When there were evidences of sincerity of purpose, all who came to Christ to be instructed, or to have their doubts removed in relation to his kingdom and its ordinances or institutions, were welcomed, and readily listened to and taught. The manner in which he gave heed to the timid inquirer was so assuring, that it was said of him " a bruised reed shall he not break, and smoking flax shall he not quench." When we are told of those whom he encountered, that he " answered them saying," we usually find that he replied to them in the manner regarded as most effective in some other schools of great celebrity, by asking questions, which either led in themselves to the confession he wished to elicit, or put the reasoners to silence through their inability to answer. His opponents were convinced at last that all their efforts to catch him in the snare of controversy were in vain; and we are told that the Pharisees, the Sadducees and scribes were successively worsted, that the tempting lawyer was silenced, and that others were confounded by the asking of the simple question, "What think ye of Christ? Whose son is he?"

The power of Christ to know the thoughts of men gave him an advantage that no other teacher ever possessed; and there are evidences of the existence of this faculty in some of the replies that are recorded, that seem rather adapted to some unrevealed circumstance connected with the enquirer than to any word spoken at the time. The insight which his divinity gave him into the exceeding sinfulness of sin, and the perfect knowledge he had of the moral position of man, "far gone from original righteousness" and with a heart "desperately wicked," gave a tone of deep solemnity to all his declarations. From the same cause, the weight of the rebukes he sometimes administered, and the severity of his condemnations, extending even to the eternal destruction of body and soul, were only a foreshadowing of the sentence he will pronounce as "Judge of all men" when seated upon the throne of doom.

In the halls of the Aryan pandits there is more that is allied to the prophets of the Jews than to the philosophers of Greece. The unseen world was to the Indian sages of paramount interest. They realised it more powerfully than the teachers of the west, thought on it more profoundly, and were greatly more elaborate in their speculations on its mysteries. The members of the pantheistic school regarding absorption into the deity as the summum bonum, taught that it is the part of a wise man to seek to free himself from all present entanglements, and thus prepare himself for deliverance from all future influences and responsibilities. This thought gave an air of great seriousness to their investigation; and enlisted the sympathies of a wide circle of persons, who were thereby interested in what they did and said. Women had then enrolled disciples, as well as men. And as the heretics incidentally introduced into the history of Buddhism are not unfrequently represented as of low origin, and yet as possessing great influence, we may infer that the acknowledged guides of the people were found among all classes and castes. The followers of the atheistic school professed to believe in nothing further than the mental phenomena of the passing moment; but as each successive moment must necessarily and unavoidably bring with it some degree of sorrow, they sought, by profound meditation, and other exercises, to prevent the continuance of existence, which they thought could be overcome by the destruction of the vitality in the seed of being, as where a grain of wheat has been subjected to the process of boiling it has lost for ever its fructifying energy.

In nearly all the schools, there were one or two more prominent tenets, that were regarded as the watch-words of the system; and there were certain forms and usages required to be observed by the postulants: but none of the great teachers of the post-Vedic ages, with whose history we are acquainted, reduced their systems of doctrine or codes of discipline to the same perfection of order as Sákya Muni. The mode in which he taught was well adapted to the nature of the circumstances under which he sought to impart instruction.*

He did not always wait for an application from those whom he saw were prepared to profit by the light of the Dharma. It was his custom to look through the world, with his divine

---

* A Brahman who was celebrating a ploughing festival, on seeing the approach of Sàyka Muni said to the attendants, "See, now, this great mendicant has come to spoil our sport. Were he to work like us who are husbandmen, he might achieve an enviable greatness; but now he does nothing: spending his time in idleness, and coming to different festivals that he may beg something to eat." Then addressing himself to Buddha, he said, "Muni, I plough and sow; and from my ploughing and sowing I receive grain, and enjoy the produce: Muni, it would be better if you were to plough and to sow, and then you would have food to eat." Buddha replied, "Brahman, I do plough and sow; and from my ploughing and sowing I reap immortal fruit." On hearing this, the Brahman thought thus: "The Muni says that he ploughs and sows; but he has neither plough nor any other instrument; he must have spoken falsely." Yet on looking at him, he thought it impossible that so comely a person could tell an untruth; and he, therefore, said, "Muni, I see no plough; no goad; no oxen; if you perform the work of a husbandman, where are your implements?" In reply Buddha informed him, that his field was the Dharma; the weeds that he plucked up, the cleaving to existence; the plough that he used, wisdom; the seed that he sowed, the seeking of purity; the work that he performed, attention to precepts; the harvest that he reaped, nirvâna; and when he had explained these matters at greater length, he exhorted the Brahman to sow in the same field, unfolding before him the advantage of obtaining an entrance to the paths that lead to the destruction of sorrow.

eyes, to see who was ready to be caught in the net of truth, and then to frame some reason for visiting the spot where the hopeful man or woman was to be found. It was not to mankind alone that wisdom was imparted, but on addressing the déwas of the heavens, he spoke to them as if they were as much under the influence of human passions as men themselves, and gave the same advices and directions, when in their presence still extolling the excellence of the Dharma. A déwa having proposed four questions to his companions, which they were unable to answer, it was agreed that the matter should be referred to Buddha.* The members of the deputation, after due reverence paid, said to him, "Which is the best mode of bestowing alms? What is more acceptable and pleasurable than anything else? What is the best mode of putting an end to sensuous desire?" To these questions he answered by one word, "the Dharma." "The giving of alms" he said "though good in itself, cannot introduce any one into the paths of deliverance. The preaching of the Dharma, and the effort to communicate it to others, were therefore, the most excellent alms. All that is in the world captivates the senses. It is but a means to plunge man the more deeply in the vortex of existence and sorrow. But the hearing of the Dharma rejoices the heart to such an extent as often to open a spring of joyful tears. It destroys all passion, and establishes man in the state of an arhat It is therefore, the most excellent of all things."

The Muni frequently took notice of passing events, that he might make them the medium of teaching some important lesson. On one occasion, having risen early that he might visit the city of Rajagaha, in order to procure alms, he saw a Brahman engaged in his devotions, with wet hair and dripping garments bending in the six directions, and worshiping the several quarters, towards which he inclined his head. When asked why he did this, he said that as his father was dying he directed him to perform this ceremony. But Buddha informed him that this was not the proper way in which to worship the six directions; and said that it was to be done by the practice of six modes of virtuous action, and by avoiding six modes of evil conduct, each of which he enumerated and explained.

When any one came to him with a good motive. however ignorant or even skilful he might be, he was listened to kindly and with patience. The opinions of the enquirer were found out by some confession drawn from his own lips, by which he was brought unconsciously to make statements, and utter sen-

* Bigandet, page 282

timents, that gradually led to an acknowledgement of the truth, and by this means it was shewn that principles were already held that could not possibly agree with the conclusions to which they were thought to lead. We have an instance of the manner in which he used a similar mode of argument, on an occasion when he exercised the congenial office of a peacemaker. Two parties belonging to his own royal race were preparing to fight, in consequence of a dispute that has had its parallel in other lands. It was about the embankment of a stream of water. On going to the combatants he said, after he had learnt the cause of the quarrel, "What is the value of water?" "It is trifling" said the princes. "What of earth?" "It is inconsiderable" "What of (the blood of) kings?" "It is unspeakably great." "Then," said he, "would you destroy that which is of unspeakable value for that which in comparison is worthless?" By this means the battle was prevented; and other princes might learn wisdom from the same lesson.

In what are called the Játakas, or Birth Stanzas, five hundred and fifty in number, a discourse is founded on some recent occurrence, on which the Muni comments, uttering some apt aphorism, and then referring to some event that took place, of a similar character, in reference to the same persons in a former state of existence. For instance, there is the verse "Fraudful cunning does not in the end produce permanent advantage. The fraudulent person may be circumvented, as the crab was by the crane." This is followed by the story of a priest who cheated another priest in relation to a robe. Upon being told of the circumstance, Buddha related the legend of a crab that by its nippers cut off the neck of a crane that intended to take his life, as he had done that of many fishes that had lived in the same pond. The verse was repeated as the moral of the story, much after the manner of our own fables, not a few of which are identical with more attributed to Sákya Muni. In some instances one story runs into another, in perplexing succession, as in the most popular of the tales translated from the Arabic, but most of them add some new feature to the narration, and contribute to the force of the maxim with which it is connected. Some of the Játakas are of considerable length.

In graver disquisitions, or in those parts of the Dharma that treat on subjects more abstract or profound, though the syllogistic form of reasoning is largely used, it is in connection with terms and distinctions, that are extended and elaborated to a degree almost incredible. These definitions are presented the most prominently in the last division of the Tripitaka, or the works founded on it. But in the manner in which the Muni is usually represented as teaching his disciples, we seem to have two men alternately before us, one eminently metaphysical in the trains of thought he pursued with the greatest earnestness, and logical in the manner in which they are presented; so that the false reasoner is entangled in the meshes of well-conducted argument, without the power to set himself free; and the other commencing with some unsound principle or mistaken postulate, lengthens out an involved discourse, with propositions that have no interest in themselves, and that are puerile in the manner of their illustration, and without practical purpose in their conclusions.

Jesus Christ is never detected in an error. He is always ready to meet the gainsayer, and even the officers of the high priests, sent on set purpose to take him, confessed to their disappointed superiors, "Never man spake like this man." In the manner of teaching said to have been adopted by the Muni, as seen in the readiness to impart knowledge, the plainness with which it was communicated, the asking of tentative questions, and the sincerity of purpose apparent in many of the discourses, there is, perhaps a nearer approach to that which is presented in the narrative of the Gospels than in any other portion of his recorded character, but there is still sufficient difference to tell at once which is the erring mortal and which the divine Instructor.

BOOK IV.

THE RULE OF LIFE.

CHAPTER I.

THE RULE OF LIFE.

In this chapter, we shall regard as coming within our province, all that concerns human conduct; all that tells the character of the inner man, as the statue or portrait would reveal his outward form. With the believer in revelation, the Rule of Life has a far wider inclusiveness than can possibly enter into the mind of the teacher whose code of morals is founded solely upon the suggestions of intuition. We learn from the word of the Lord that there are two great classes of obligation that are binding upon all intelligent creatures; their duty towards God, the Creator, and their duty to the beings that are the workmanship of the Creator's hand. In addition, when our responsibility to God is acknowledged, an entirely new phase, and one that involves consequences the most serious, is given to the whole economy of existence. It becomes, unspeakably greater in its importance: and no code of moral law can be perfect in which this principle is overlooked, or in which it is made to hold a secondary place.

In the revelations of Christ there is a further individuality. The unsoiling of the soul is not necessarily by a gradual process. It may be accomplished by a specific act, in its exercise of universal influence. When man has to work out his own salvation, without the working within him of the sanctifying influences of the Holy Spirit, he must slowly approach the citadel of evil, contesting with the enemy for every inch of ground he gains. He has to confess, "When I would do good evil is present with me." But when aided by God, the soldier of the cross can overcome all antagonisms, whether from within or without, as by a cóup de main. He has yet to fight; but if he is faithful to the grace that will be communicated to him, in his new position, victory will be as frequent as battle. Hence, Jesus Christ had no school for the teaching of the individual disciple, who was to be led on slowly from the rudiments of the Gospel to instruction in the whole truth. As he said to the blind man, "See!" and he saw, and to the leper, "Be clean!" and he was cleansed, there and then: so he asserted the possession of a power upon earth, to say to the contrite spirit that believed in him, "Thy sins are forgiven thee" and it was declared by the Forerunner that he was the Lamb of God, "which taketh away the sin of the world" On this account, his commands were issued with authority, and the promise of aid to accomplish all that was inculcated was given at the same time as the decree. "If thine eye be single, thy whole body shall be full of light." "Make the tree good, and his fruit good; for the tree is known by his fruit." When the fountain is made clean, all that proceeds from it partakes of its clearness: its natural outflow is purity. And until this is accomplished, all appearances of reformation are too much like the green weed that spreads itself over the mud of the treacherous morass, hiding its foulness, and even giving to it a degree of attractiveness, but leaving it still, in reality a dirty, deceitful, noxious swamp.

The constancy of the attention of Christ to these principles must never be lost sight of by those who seek to form a correct estimate of the power of the Gospel as a purifier of morals. It meets us at all stages of the Saviour's ministry, from its commencement. "Except a man be born again, he cannot see the kingdom of God." The old man is to be slain, and a new spirit to be communicated, as different to the former one as life from death. There are to be new motives, new powers, new pursuits, new aims. Outcast man is to be raised from his state of degradation; his presence is no longer to be a pollution; and there is to be granted to him the privilege of adoption into the holy family of God, with all its rights, immunities, dignities, and wealth of inheritance. The glory of that possession far transcends all that the apostles were led to expect at the time when they were called upon to separate themselves from all secular pursuits, and follow Christ. They were told that when their faithfulness had been proved, they were to "sit upon twelve thrones, judging the twelve tribes of Israel." The glory upon which they had once fixed their vision was never to be realised after the manner they had supposed, in the earthliness of their uninformed imaginations, but they were to attain to far higher privilege: not to be mere servitors in God's realms, but themselves to be invested with the rectoral office, sitting upon thrones of judgment.

The grandeur of the aim of Christ was seen in the fact, that his commands were not to be regarded as of local or limited obligation. Even when denouncing local customs, the condemnation was to be understood as unfolding principles of general importance. This limitlessness of area was recognized throughout the whole range of his utterances. "Except ye repent, ye shall all likewise perish." "What I say unto you, I say unto all, Watch." "And I, if I be lifted up from the earth will draw all men after me." "God so loved the world, that he gave his only begotten Son, that whosoever believeth in him should not perish, but have everlasting life."

At the commencement of our Lord's ministry it was announced, that no part of the old law was to be abrogated. "I am not come to destroy, but to fulfil." Not one jot or tittle was to pass from it, until all had been perfected. All its requirements were to be transferred to the laws of the new kingdom; all its prohibitions were equally to be regarded; and the whole system of its rewards and punishments was to be equally operative and influential. Its power was increasingly fortified by stern reproof of the attempts that had been made to weaken it, and the evil designs of the men were unsparingly exposed who had sought to make it utter mandates that were not in accordance with the will of God. The sect most earnest in upholding its forms were told that their zeal was not accepted; and the multitude learnt that unless they secured a righteousness exceeding that of the Pharisees there was no entrance for them into the kingdom of heaven. There was significance in the words he uttered, and often repeated, "I say unto you." He was not simply a corrector of abuses; an asserter only of the original precept, just a restorer of the primitive canon, and nothing more. He assumed a right that had been claimed by no previous interpreter, and that no one had asserted in the "old time" of which he spoke. The people acknowledged the authority with which he addressed them but their hearts were waxed gross, and they did not perceive that in his discourse on the mount he had uplifted morality to a higher position than any it had previously occupied, not only as taught from the chair of the scribe but in the school of the most enlightened prophet. There may be perfectness of propriety as to the outward conduct, and blamelessness of life, whilst, in the sight of God there is fatal deficiency and even much depravity. There may be murder, without the movement of a muscle; theft, without the abstraction of the smallest possession; and adultery, without the least approach towards outward criminality. It is the heart that God looks upon, as the source whence the motive proceeds, that may vitiate what has the look of innocence and render that which has the semblance of purity exceedingly sinful. When Christ had asserted the supremacy of the law, and explained the spirituality of its meaning, he proceeded to operate upon the heart as a skilful sculptor works upon the clay in which he is forming his model, preparing it to receive the impress of the divine hand.

Jesus Christ was the first teacher who gave to woman her rightful position. We are introduced to her in his discourses as she grinds at the mill, casts her leaven into the meal, joins in the marriage procession, and rejoices the bridegroom as his bride. He would have man look at her as it was intended that he should "from the beginning." Those were grand words of God, when he said, "I will make him a help meet for him." This was to be her privilege for ever. She was to be "a help" to man. The former part of these words of solemn consecration he remembers—"A help;" but he forgets the other part, the thought linked with it, wedded to it from the moment he first saw her in her primal beauty, "a help meet," meet to help: not, as in nearly all places away from the hearing of the voice of Christ, to do all the hard work of the world alone, "a help meet for him" worthy to be his second self; not only bone of his bone, but soul of his soul, with one warm heart and one brave hope. She first seen after the fall prepares us for woman's subsequent history. In man's ungenerous attempt to throw the blame of the transgression on the woman, she saw what she would have to expect when the gate of Paradise was closed. And yet there seems to be mercy to the woman in the sentence passed upon the man. "Thorns also and thistles shall the ground bring forth to thee. In the sweat of thy face shalt thou eat bread." It was evidently intended that man should do all the severe toil. It was his hand that was to be pierced by the thorn, and it was he who was to expose himself to the scratch of the thistle; and thus make the work of the world so far pleasant to the woman. It was his turn to be the help-meet; the bread winner; the woman ruler, but exercising his authority so gently and lovingly that, according to God's holy ordinance he shall still be the desire of the woman's heart. Women of all classes are connected with the history of Christ. He was born of a pure virgin; he raised from the dead one of the maidens of Israel, about twelve years of age; a sick woman was healed of her infirmity by touching the hem of his garment; a poor woman was commended because she had cast into the treasury more than all the rest; "for they did cast in of the abundance, but she of her want did cast in all that she had, even all her living." Well may the females of India say, as they listen to the word of God when read to them in their zenanas by their fair sisters from the west, "Your bible is a woman's bible; our religious books say nothing of woman but what is cruel, but your bible is full of kind and loving words towards us."

The whole life of Christ was one continued didactic discourse. In his own person was exemplified perfectly all he taught; and the spotless beauty of his character has so struck the sceptic, that he has been led to acknowledge its grandeur in words eloquent as the voices of heaven. Though himself without sin, it was his study to render assistance to sinful men, helping their infirmities, bringing into activity the hope that the world would have crushed out and destroyed, and breathing health and power into spirits ready to droop and give way to despair. The apostle sums up the whole series of his benevolent acts by saying, "he went about doing good." No one but "the Greeks that came up to worship at the feast," and who knew him not, ever seemed afraid to approach him, or to enter into conversation with him, or to seek his advice, or to ask for his assistance. But one sight of the living loving man will tell more than many sentences of exposition. The mothers of Israel ventured to request that he would put his hands upon their children. The little ones themselves seem to have been eager to attract his notice, and the permission had not to be given them in these terms, "Then bring them to me;" or "Send them;" but "Suffer them to come," as if they were already anxious to come to the Saviour; so attractive was his presence. There was none of the moroseness too often assumed by the successful teacher; nor of the awe that usually accompanies the man who exercises the power of working miracles. "Forgive and be forgiven," "Love and be beloved," were precepts, with an accompanying promise and privilege. In the all embracing arms of his own affection were expressly included his enemies and persecutors; publicans, sinners, and Samaritans. The love that he taught and upon the constant exercise of which he insisted, was not to be cribbed and confined to each man's own caste, or guild, or school, or creed, or nation, but to be so expansive as to reach the whole estate of universal man.

The word Gospel, though not used in the Old Testament, must have had a definite meaning before the coming of Christ, as he appeared before the Jews saying, "Repent, and believe the gospel." The perfect church of the Gospel was not formed before the resurrection; but its platform was prepared and its foundation laid, deep and broad. "Upon this rock, I will build, (oikodomésó) my church." The Holy Ghost was to collect the living stones of the temple about to be erected. It was by his hand that they were to be polished, and placed in situ, and it was through his presence that the intended shrine was to be filled with the divine glory. "But the Holy Ghost was not yet given because that Jesus was not yet glorified." To see the temple in its full majesty we must turn towards the writings of the apostles, and to know all the "peace" and "good will" proceeding therefrom, we must visit every land where it has been received in its integrity. This broad view would, however take us beyond the limits to which we have proposed to confine ourselves, and we must be content with saying that it is the aim of Christ's religion to make all men, everywhere, and always, happy and holy; putting away from the practice of men all things connected with tyranny and oppression; making them willing to bear the burdens of each other, by extending the hand of help, wherever it is needed or will be welcome; banishing from the earth all that is cold or churlish and that partakes of narrowness of mind or heart: and so changing the human heart that every act of the Christian man shall be honest in the sight of God, and kind towards his fellow man, and even his thoughts ever pure, and free from semblance of guile or guise. This is the morality of the gospel of the Son of God.

It is in the comparative superiority of its moral code that the principal excellence of the Dharma is supposed to consist; and we enter upon our examination of its ethical character with no disposition to depreciate its work or deny the advantages it has conferred upon India and the nations further east. By the adoption of this course we think that we promote the interests of truth. Revelation tells us, that "when the Gentiles which have not the law, do by nature [phusei in their natural state, unaided by an immediate revelation] the things contained in the law, these having not the law, are a law unto themselves; which shew the work of the law written in their hearts, their conscience also bearing witness, and their thoughts, the mean while, accusing or else excusing one another." The moral state of the heathen world proves most clearly the necessity of a divine revelation; but both from the writings of their ancient sages, and the conversations recorded by our modern missionaries as having taken place between them and the Buddhists of India and the heathen of other lands, there appears a sense of right and wrong sometimes dim and feeble, but often felt by them in a painful and oppressive degree: and this, whilst it is a proof of the good-will of God towards all his intelligent creatures, indicates his justice in making them amenable to a general judgment. The mercy of God becomes more apparent according to the extent of light that men receive, but the punitive justice that he exercises is seen to be righteous, from the same cause. Even when the existence of God is denied, or entirely unknown, the conscience exists, and asserts its claims, and in numberless instances it is successfully appealed to, to convince men of the evil of sin and the necessity of an atonement.

If the axiom we have previously laid down be correct, that no system of morals can be perfect in which the existence of an intelligent Supreme Being is not recognized, as the source of all law and obligation, everywhere present and regardful of the acts of all his creatures to whom he has given a moral sense, then must Buddhism be regarded, without further investigation, as a religion destitute of the requisite authority; not as a religion in the strict sense, but as system of ethics. In the Dharma there is properly speaking, no lawgiver, and therefore no law. There are precepts given by Sákya Muni; but he is not himself their originator; he merely makes known what he regards as eternal truths; but who first declared them, or by what authority they are now rendered obligatory, we are not informed. With him, sin is not sin, as it is not the transgression of a law. It is an inconvenience but little more. We may infer that it is an evil and it may be a pollution, but there is nothing about it that implies guilt. The power to declare what is good and what is evil was first received by Buddha as he sat at the foot of the bo-tree, and was the result of his "all knowingness," which was itself the result of the entire destruction of all cleaving to sensuous objects, or the overcoming of all evil desire. "As a [supreme] Buddha, he acknowledges no teacher, admits of no inspiration or revelation from a higher source; but declares himself to be the fountain of knowledge for all existing beings, whatever may be their dignity." But upon his own principles, we may refuse to acknowledge his authority, as so far from bring all wise, he betrays ignorance and mistakes upon almost every subject about which his supposed opinions are recorded.

When inquiry was made from Christ as to the way of preparation for eternal life, he said, "What is written in the law?" meaning, as we learn from the context, the law of God. At other times, there were his words, "I say unto you;" but he declared that what he said was by the authority of the Father, with whom he was "one." "The word which ye hear is not mine, but the Father's which sent me." The commands of Christ were, therefore the commands of God, whose right it is to rule, and who requires a loving obedience from all his creatures, to be ceaselessly presented, and bringing to its exercise every affection of the heart, and the utmost earnestness of soul. "The Father hath committed all judgment unto the

Son." In the discourse on the mount he exclaimed, "Whosoever therefore shall break one of these least commandments, and shall teach men so, he shall be called the least in the kingdom of heaven." With this compare the words of James. "Whosoever shall keep the whole law, and yet offend in one point, he is guilty of all." The law of God requires perfect obedience, and no power that is less than divine can rescind, or revoke any of its precepts, or alter them in the least degree. They are fixed, as God's immutability; extended, in their requirements, as the authority of God; and include all times, places and persons. The ordinances of Buddha, as we have seen are not imperative commands. The observance of them implies no deserving; the non-observance of them no criminality. In the Dharma there is no such sentence as this: "The Lord is longsuffering, and of great mercy, forgiving iniquity and transgression, and sin, and by no means clearing the guilty."

CHAPTER II.

THE ECONOMY OF THE CHURCH.

In the conversation that was held by Christ with the woman of Samaria, as he sat by Jacob's well, weary with his journey which must have been over miles of limestone rock, exposed to the intense glare of the sun, as it was then the hour of noon, he re-asserted a truth too long forgotten, that had been acknowledged not far from the same spot, in the distant past. Another wearied pilgrim—the same whose name had been given to the well by which Jesus sat—coming from a locality further south, saw a vision of God, not at noon, but in the night; not near to a frequented pathway, but in the loneliness of utter solitude. When Jacob awoke out of his sleep, he said, "Surely the Lord is in this place and I knew it not!" And he was afraid, and said, "How dreadful to this place; this is none other but the house of God, and this is the gate of heaven!" The spangling of the roof of that hallowed house had only the stars for its adornment, for the sun had set when he lighted upon that place; the veil that was drawn aside in the soft roseate blush of the morning was the receding darkness in the midst of which he had slept, as his head lay upon a pillow of stone and the solemn hush that rested everywhere, as if preparing the world for the rest of a Sabbath day, were all scenes presented in the wilderness; yet the shekinah was there; it was "the house of God," and "the gate of heaven." Had men been willing to learn the important lesson thus taught, they would have seen that the whole earth is one consecrated temple of Jehovah, and that in any part of it they may hold holy converse with God; but the Israelites sought to confine the privilege to Jerusalem and the Samaritans to Gerizim, near the shadow of which Christ was then set. They mistook the restriction on sacrifice for a restriction on worship. Greatly must it have puzzled "Samaria's daughter," when Christ said, "The hour cometh, when ye shall neither in this mountain [exclusively] nor yet at Jerusalem, worship the Father...The hour cometh, and now is when the true worshippers shall worship the Father in spirit and in truth: for the Father seeketh such to worship him. God is a Spirit; and they that worship him, must worship him in spirit and in truth." This was the old truth, more clearly affirmed, taught in the vision seen by the wanderer whom the woman called "our father Jacob." It was evident, therefore, that the kingdom to be established by Christ, was not to be local in its influence or limited in its extent by mountains or seas, the usual termini of nationality. Both Jesus and the woman spoke of "worship," and of that alone. There was no mention of sacrifice, or of any other rite. There was not, indeed at any time, a formal abrogation of sacrifice; but the character of the future had been already revealed. It had been shewn, inferentially, first, that the sacrifice of a slain animal was no longer needed when drawing nigh to God; and then that its continuance would not be possible, in conformity with the old canon. Christ had said to his disciples, "Where two or three are gathered together in my name there am I in the midst of them." When he afterwards sent them forth, he said, "Go ye, into all the world, and preach the gospel to every creature. He that believeth and is baptised shall be saved." They were to preach the gospel, everywhere and to all people, and the Lord promised to be with them alway. In the terms of their commission, there was no mention of any observance that had been in force connected with the Mosaic dispensation. If the passover for instance, was to be kept, it could not be after the old manner, as it would have taken half a lifetime, for some of the members of the church to have gone from their own homes to the locality of which it was said, that it was the "place where the Lord shall choose to place his name there;" and which was the only spot in the whole world where the paschal lamb was permitted to be slain. At the period of the crucifixion there was the occurrence of a significant event; perplexing to the Jews; but most instructive to the follows of Him who then expired upon the cross. "The veil of the temple," that no one could pass but the high priest alone and he only on one festival of the year, "was rent in twain from the top to the bottom." We see the importance of baptism as an initial rite to be received of all men who would enter into Christ's church, in the accounts that are given of the struggles carried on in the minds of many of the heathen, when their sincerity is thereby tested, and the soul has to be wrenched at once from all that is held dear upon earth, and all forsaken for Christ. But though this significant ordinance, first brought into prominent notice by John, was to be continued, there was an effectual bar placed upon the repetition of the service of the Levitical priesthood. Christ had said of the temple, "There shall not be left here one stone upon another, that shall not be thrown down." He had previously called it "his Father s house;" but he now called it "your house," and said, "Your house is left unto you desolate;" and desolate it was to remain, until they were prepared to say, "Blessed is he that cometh in the name of the Lord." It was plain, therefore, that the head of the kingdom was not to be Jerusalem, and that the priesthood was not to be confined to the sons of Aaron.

There were not more than two occasions on which the Messiah spoke particularly of the church. On the former of the two, he said to the apostle whom he had first called, "Thou art Peter, and upon this rock I will build my church, and the gates of hell shall not prevail against it." From these words we learn, 1. that Christ was about to establish a church; 2 that it would be opposed by the legions of hell; 3. that this opposition would not prevail; and, 4. that it was to be built upon something connected with, or represented by, Peter. That it should be built upon Peter personally was not possible. The meaning must, therefore, be a figurative one and may declare that the church was to be built, i e. proceed from, or be commenced by Peter, in his official capacity: or it may declare that it was to be built upon the confession he had just made that Christ was "the Son of the living God." At this time, as upon so many other occasions, Peter was regarded as the representative of the twelve. Both immediately before and after the confession the word "ye" is used, and in the confession that was made as well as the charge received, all the apostles were included. The keys of the kingdom were connected with the power of binding and loosing; as was afterwards more clearly explained by Christ, when he said, the other apostles being present, "Receive ye the Holy Ghost: whose soever sins ye remit, they are remitted unto them, and whose soever sins ye retain they are retained." With the Jews there was the complaint that one school loosed, and another bound; but as Christ breathed upon all the disciples, and to all imparted the guidance of the Spirit, in one and the same manner, there could be no similar variance between the doctrines they taught, or the discipline they exercised. We learn from these revelations that the church of Christ is to be founded on and ever linked to, the confession of Peter; and we may learn, further, that where this faith is not, the church of Christ is not. It is to endure for ever, for "the gates of hell," the power of Hades, "shall not prevail against it."

The notices given by Christ previous to his death, of his intended church, are few and indefinite. Knowing that it was to extend far and to exist to distant ages, it appears singular that more specific rules were not formed for its government. When we look at the position of the church as it appears on the day of the resurrection and at the state of the world, it seems impossible that so feeble a cause can succeed in the battle it will forthwith have to commence, in order to gain influence and authority. But we may learn thereupon two lessons: 1. That the power of the Gospel was not regarded by its Author as consisting in the form of its ecclesiastical government, or in any system of hierarchical polity. Otherwise Christ, in his infinite wisdom, would have made authoritative arrangement for the early settlement of all the more important church questions. 2. Christ must have foreseen the certain accomplishment of the promise he had given that the Holy Ghost would be communicated to the apostles, in a greater degree than that in which His power had rested upon them whilst their Master was yet with them; joining these thoughts together, we may discover the reason why it was not seen to be necessary by Christ that the church should be definitely constituted, or its polity authoritatively defined, before his death. But we learn from Matthew xviii. 20 that it was to be connected with a particular form of faith, a belief in the divinity of the Son of God. The Apostles, in order that it might be established were to preach and baptize, but in what manner they were to ordain other apostles, or by whom the gospel was to be taken to those parts of "the world" they could not personally visit, was not specially revealed. Immediately previous to his death, Christ instituted another ordinance, that has been regarded, with a few exceptions by all Christians, as of universal obligation, called in Scripture, "the Lord's Supper." But even here, we have no positive direction as to the persons by whom it was to be administered, though we learn that all were to partake of it, and we know that the blood represented by the wine to be poured out and drunk was to be shed for "the many," and that all believers are as much interested in it as the apostles to whom the command was first given. The time, place and form of celebration was left to be arranged by the officers of the church, according to circumstances; but there is no authority for the mystery that has been thrown around it by men who would assume the priesthood in a church in which there can be only one Priest, Jesus Christ, who is both Offerer and Host, and the same men would change a simple rite into a histrionic perfomance and a gorgeous superstition.

The followers of Christ were not yet prepared for the establishment of a church that was to be permanent in its form and constitution: the elements to form it were not yet in existence in many places: and if the power of the gospel had consisted in anything outward or human, its existence would have been imperilled when Jesus was taken up to heaven. But there was the rich legacy of promise previously given to the disciples; and in the fifty days of prayer and supplication, their memories would go back to the instructions they had received from Christ. Every word that each apostle could remember would be added to the general store, as a priceless treasure; and among them would doubtless be, the words he had spoken about binding and loosing; the retaining of sin, and the remitting; the coming of the Comforter, by whom they were to be led into the way of all truth, and the constancy of the Saviour's presence, that was to accompany them "even unto the end of the world!"

Under the guidance of the same divine Spirit, the apostles appointed "bishops and deacons," or as they are sometimes called, "elders and deacons;" gifts were communicated "with the laying on of the hands of the presbytery;" and to Timothy this charge was given by Paul: "The things that thou hast heard of me among many witnesses, the same commit thou to faithful men, who shall be able to teach others also."

The existence of the church, even if it were nothing more than a simple *ekklésia* would necessitate a number of arrangements, such as, the authority to call it, the preparation of a place in which to hold it, the rules to be observed in conducting it, and a reason would have to be assigned why it was called together; but though with it there was to be connected also preaching and teaching, the administration of the sacraments, the exercise of discipline and the adjustment of other matters of high importance; beyond certain rudimentary principles, neither in the gospels nor the epistles, is there presented so distinct an outline that it will be at once recognized as the intended form of the future church. But this matter does not fall within our province for exhaustive discussion, as we confine ourselves almost exclusively to the times of Christ. As to the doctrines to be taught, all possible pains were to be taken to preserve and present them in their original purity without any addition whatever from unauthorized sources; so that the apostle of the Gentiles said: "Though we or an angel from heaven preach any other gospel unto you than that which we have preached unto you let him be accursed;" and the apostle John said, "Whosoever transgresseth, and abideth not in the doctrine of Christ, hath not God. He that abideth in the doctrine of Christ, he hath both the Father and the Son. If there come any unto you and bring not this doctrine, receive him not into your house, neither bid him God speed. For he that biddeth him God speed is partaker of his evil deeds." 2 John 9, 10.

The ecclesiastical arrangements of Sákya Muni are in many respects, just the reverse of those of Jesus Christ. He was comparatively careless about doctrine, but there are given in his name the most minute directions as to the discipline to be observed by those who sought to receive the full benefit of the Dharma From the date of its establishment, there is throughout one radical difference The commands of Christ were binding upon all men : the privileges of the gospel were to be shared by all. In what concerns the inner life, and power over sin, the evidence of acceptance with God, freedom of access to the throne of the heavenly grace, and the full assurance of hope in relation to a glorious immortality, no difference was made between the layman and the priest; in the gospel there was no esoteric school, founded upon ecclesiastical position, no path of privilege into which men were officially permitted to enter. But the aid to be received from the teaching of the Muni was of little or no avail to those who did not possess previous merit; it had no power to prevent the consequence of sin; and its highest position of privilege could only be attained by those who formally abandoned the world, and took upon themselves the profession of a religious life, which was connected with restraints that prevented the possibility of its being universally embraced. All could not carry the alms-bowl, or where were the alms-giver? All could not preserve strict continence, or how was the race to be perpetuated?

The laws of profession were modified, as circumstances arose that necessitated an alteration in their form. This was brought forward as an argument against the power of the Muni to see into the future; but it was replied, that a physician may be perfectly acquainted with the properties of all kinds of medicinal preparations, but he does not administer them previously to the appearance of the disease; so, though Buddha knew all things, he did not forbid certain practices until the necessity arose for their prohibition. To this elasticity, the system has been indebted for its continuance during so many centuries, and under circumstances so diversified. Had it been a product of abstract thought, and not of actual experience, or had it been propounded as perfect and unchangeable, from the beginning, without the power of adaptation or alteration, its immobility would have been its destruction. In these arrangements, the Muni displayed a correct knowledge of human nature, as there was in them a wise preparation for future contingencies, that from the first, was seen to be a great conservative power.

In illustration of the manner in which these arrangements were carried into effect, we may instance what was done in reference to the ordination of the monks, and the appointment of the various officers who were required for their guidance and government. The heads of the religion are commonly called priests by European writers, but Buddhism admits of no proper priesthood ; and when we use the word ordination, and other church terms, it must be understood that they are used in a sense consistent with the system, and not in their more modern acceptation. The doctrines of Buddha are not arranged systematically in any one discourse; but are to be found in detached sermons and different books ; nor was his criminal and ecclesiastical code formed at once, but enacted as circumstances occurred. At the first many of the monks being uninstructed, were slovenly in their dress; they solicited alms in an improper manner and were noisy and rude in conversation. The people were displeased at this conduct, and loudly expressed their disapprobation. The more modest monks, also, were aggrieved by it, and reported the circumstances to the Muni, who convened a chapter, censured the offenders, and issued the following precept : "Monks, I permit (or direct) that there should be spiritual superiors." He then defines the relative duties of the superior and the co-resident. The superior is to regard the other as his son, and the co-resident is to regard the superior as his father ; and they are mutually to respect and honour each other. Some of the co-residents having refused to perform their duty to the superiors, the Muni decreed : "It is not proper, monks, that a co-resident should not perform his duty to his superior. He who does not do his duty is guilty of an offence requiring confession and absolution." They still remaining disobedient, the Muni decreed : "I permit, monks, that the disobedient shall be suspended (from his position as co-resident)." He was then to be placed under discipline. The superior might declare by words, or intimate by signs, "I suspend you," or he might say, "Return not to this place," or, "Take away your alms-bowl and robes ;" or, "I have no need of your service." When any of these forms were used, the co-resident was suspended. A co-resident, who was thus suspended, not seeking reconciliation, it was decreed : "I direct, monks, that those who are suspended shall not remain without seeking forgiveness. He who does not seek forgiveness is guilty of an offence." Some superiors, on forgiveness being requested, refusing to be reconciled, he decreed: "I direct, monks, that forgiveness be granted" Still, some of the superiors would not forgive, and the co-residents, being discouraged, left the community, and joined themselves to other religious orders. Upon this, Buddha decreed: "It is not proper, monks, to refuse forgiveness when it is solicited. He who refuses to forgive is guilty of an offence." Some preceptors having suspended the obedient and permitted the disobedient to remain without suspension, on the fact being reported, Buddha decreed: "Monks, it is improper to suspend those who do their duty. He who does so is guilty of the first offence. It is improper not to suspend those who neglect their duty. He who does not place such under suspension is guilty of the first offence." Five reasons are assigned why a pupil may be placed under suspension. If he does not manifest proper affection, attachment and respect to his preceptor, or if he is without modesty of deportment, or neglects his studies.

There were at that time monks of more than ten years standing who were unwise and unlearned, and who yet received other monks as pupils. In consequence of this, in some instances the preceptor was ignorant and the pupil learned, and much discontent arose; both monks and people complaining of the impropriety. But when Buddha had investigated the circumstances, he reproved the offenders, and decreed: "Monks, a person who is unwise and incompetent shall not receive a resident pupil. I permit wise and competent monks, of ten or more years standing to receive resident pupils."

Some of the superiors and preceptors having left their former place of residence, and others having left the priesthood or joined other fraternities, and some having died, the monks did not know how far they were released from the duty of attending upon them. The subject was brought to the notice of Buddha who decreed: "Monks, for these five reasons, a monk is released from the duty of living with his superior. If the superior remove to another place; if he leave the priesthood; if he die; if he join some other fraternity; or if he give leave of absence."

Buddha then defined the qualifications necessary to be possessed by those who become superiors, preceptors, or who have novices under them. "He should be perfect in moral virtue (i. e. without any need of further instruction or advice respecting virtue), in meditation, in wisdom, in deliverance from desire, and in the knowledge resulting from that deliverance. He must also be able to establish others in the same virtues and excellencies."

As these are qualities possessed only by the arhats, or those delivered from the bonds of existence, and as, for many centuries, no monk has attained to this perfection, the above rule is not binding at present, but the following qualifications are still required: He must be orthodox, modest and grave in his deportment, diligent, wise, able to instruct his pupils and resolve their doubts, well acquainted with the rules of ecclesiastical discipline, free from ecclesiastical censure, and of ten or more years standing in the profession.

One who had been a member of another body of teachers became a monk; but disputing the doctrines taught by his superior, he left the fraternity and returned to the society to which he formerly belonged. Afterwards he came back, and requested admission as a Buddhist monk; but the case being brought before Buddha, he decreed: "Monks, if any one who has been a member of another body of teachers shall become a monk, and disputing the doctrines taught by his superior, unite himself again to the body to which he formerly belonged: should he return he must not be re-admitted to the higher profession."

Should any one, formerly a member of another body of teachers, have a desire to embrace this doctrine and discipline, to become a monk and embrace the higher profession, he shall be received on probation for four months. The permission shall be granted as follows:

First, having caused the head and beard to be shaven, and a yellow garment to be put on, the candidate shall remove his garment from one shoulder, worship the feet of the monks, and kneeling down, say with uplifted hands, "I take refuge in Buddha, I take refuge in the Dharma, I take refuge in the Sangha, the associated priesthood. A second time, I take refuge in Buddha, the Dharma, and the Sangha. A third time, I take refuge in Buddha, the Dharma and the Sangha."

Then, the candidate shall come to the Sangha, remove his garment from one shoulder, worship the feet of the monks and kneeling down say with uplifted hands, "Lords, I, N—, have been a member of such a body of teachers, I desire to receive this doctrine and discipline, and to obtain the higher profession. Lords, I request four months' probation." A second and a third time he is to make this request. A fluent and a learned priest shall then make this known to the Sangha, saying, "Hear me, my lord the Sangha, this person, formerly a member of another body of teachers, desires to receive this doctrine and discipline, and to obtain the higher profession. He requests to be admitted to a probation of four months. If it be a convenient time for the Sangha, the Sangha will admit this person, formerly a member of another body of teachers to a probation of four months. This is the proposition. The Sangha grants a probation of four months to this person, formerly a member of another body of teachers. If any venerable one consents to grant four months' probation to this person, formerly a member of another body of teachers, let him remain silent. If he do not consent let him speak. Probation for four months is given by the Sangha to this person, formerly a member of another body of teachers. The Sangha consents, and therefore is silent, and thus I receive it."

Buddha then explains the reason of this proceeding, arising from the habits of these teachers of other bodies; viz, that they visit the houses for alms at unseasonable hours (when the women may be careless as to their dress, or the exposure of their persons); that they resort for alms to places where there are loose women, widows, and grown-up girls, or when there are catamites or female ascetics; that they are loud and overbearing in conversation; not careful in what ought to engage their attention; indolent, inquisitive, not under control, dull in understanding, lose their temper when the doctrines they hold are controverted, and speak against Buddha, the Dharma and the Sangha. He then states, that if they continue thus, they ought not to receive the higher profession at the end of their probation.

He also directs, that if the person who seeks to be admitted on probation be a nude ascetic, the superior shall supply him with garments, and see to his head being shaved; that if any ascetic with clotted hair, or a fire-worshipper, seek admission to the order, he may be admitted without probation as their doctrines are correct respecting the results of moral conduct; and that any one who is of the Sákya race is to have the same privilege, although he may have been a member of another body of teachers; and that he concedes this to them as being of the same race as himself.

At one period great sickness prevailed in Mágadha, especially from leprosy, ulcers, eruptions of various kinds, consumption, and epilepsy; these were named the five (principal) diseases. A number of persons sought the aid of the king's physician, offering him the whole of their property, and even to become his slaves, if he would undertake their cure. The physician replied, that he could not possibly attend to them, his duty to the king, the royal household, to Buddha and his monks, who were placed under his care by the king, occupying the whole of his time. Upon this some of the men determined to join the fraternity, that they might obtain the aid of the royal physician. They accordingly went to the Sangha, and were admitted to profession. Being monks, the physician prescribed for them, and they were restored to health. After this, they left the fraternity. The physician meeting one of them recognized him, and said, "Were you not a monk?" He acknowledged it, and stated that he had become a monk solely to obtain his aid as a physician, and that upon being cured he had returned to his family. The physician was much displeased, and complained to Buddha, requesting him to prohibit those who had then diseases from being admitted as monks. Buddha soothed his mind with religious discourse, and upon his departure, decreed:

"Monks, it is not proper to admit into the order any person who is afflicted with the five diseases. He who admits such a person is guilty of the first offence."

Disturbances having broken out in the provinces, the king of Mágadha ordered his troops to quell them. Some of the warriors thought, that if they went, delighting in war, they would commit sin, and bring much demerit upon themselves; by what means shall we escape, so as to avoid committing sin, and be able to perform good works? The monks are good and virtuous men; if we join them, our object will be accomplished. They accordingly applied to the Sangha, and were admitted to profession. But when the commander of the forces enquired where such and such persons were, he was informed that they had become monks. Upon learning this, he was much displeased, and reported the case to the king, stating that such persons ought to be capitally punished, together with those who admitted them to profession.

The king, upon this, waited on the Muni, and said, "There are in my kingdom persons destitute of faith and strongly disposed to injure the monks, so it will be well for them not to admit into their order any person belonging to the king's forces." When the king was gone, Buddha called the priests together, stated the case, and decreed:

"Monks, no person in the king's pay shall be made a monk. He who admits such a person is guilty of the first offence."

The noted thief, Ángulimála, was admitted as a monk; but the people on seeing him, were alarmed and terrified, and fled away to other places, which caused extreme dissatisfaction; but when the monks reported it to Buddha, he decreed:

"Monks, no outlawed felon shall be admitted to profession; he who admits him is guilty of the first offence."

The king had commanded that no violence should be offered to any of the monks of Buddha, as they were holy and virtuous men. On one occasion, a thief had been cast into prison; but he breaking out of prison, escaped, and obtained admission as a monk. He was afterwards recognized; but when some persons went to apprehend him, they were reminded of the king's command. The people murmured, and said, "These sons of Sákya are privileged to do what they like. Why do they admit thieves who have broken out of prison?" Upon being informed of this, Buddha decreed:

"Monks, no thief who has broken out of prison shall be admitted by you; for he who admits him is guilty of the first offence."

Under similar circumstances the following laws were enacted:

No proclaimed thief shall be admitted into the order.

No person who has been flogged by a judicial sentence, shall be admitted.

No person who has been branded by a judicial sentence, shall be admitted.

No person who is in debt shall be admitted.

No person who is a slave shall be admitted. He who admits any of these persons is guilty of the first offence.

The son of a goldsmith having quarelled with his parents, went to the monastery, and was admitted as a novice. His parents enquired of the monks if they had seen such a lad there. They, not being aware of what had occurred, said that they had not seen him. After further search, he was found, he having been admitted as a novice. The parents loudly complained that the priests were shameless liars. It would seem that the monks then admitted novices on their own responsibility, without any reference to the Sangha, regularly assembled. To prevent such irregularities, when the case was reported to Buddha, he decreed:

"I direct, monks, that the shaving of the head shall be reported to the Sangha."

In consequence of this law, whenever a youth is to be admitted as a novice, the Sangha is to be assembled, and the circumstances stated to the meeting prior to the head of the candidate being shaved.

There were in Rajagaha seventeen children who were friends, Upáli being the principal of them. His parents thought much about a profession for him, by which he might obtain his livelihood after their death. They thought of his being a scribe, but remembered that writing tires the fingers. Then of his being an accountant, but that would be injurious to his chest; and were he to become a painter, that would try his eyes. They then reflected that the sons of Sákya were virtuous men; that they were well fed and comfortably clothed, and that it would be desirable to make him a priest. Upáli being pleased with the intention of his parents, went to his young friends, and proposed that they all should become monks. They replied, "If you, Upáli, become a monk, we also will become monks;" and each child requested his parent's permission to join the order. The whole of the parents were pleased with the proposition, and took them to the monks, who admitted them as novices. In the night they became restless, and cried for gruel and something to eat, and though the priests tried to pacify them, it was without success. The Muni, on hearing the noise, enquired the reason. Ananda informed him; on which he assembled the priests, and enquired if they had admitted to profession those whom they knew to be under twenty years of age. They acknowledged that they had done so; but he reproved them, stating that youths under twenty years of age were not able to endure the hardships connected with being monks, and decreed:

"Monks, it is not proper to admit to profession one who is known to be less than twenty years of age. Whoever admits such a person is guilty of the first offence."

A whole family, except the father and a male child, having died, they became monks, and went out together to collect food. When food was given to the father, the child was heard to say, "Father, give me some!" which caused the people to murmur and insinuate that the sons of Sákya were incontinent The other monks reported the case to Buddha, who decreed:

"Monks, it is not proper that a child under five years of age should be admitted to profession; he who admits him is guilty of the first offence."

A pious and faithful family who had ministered to Ananda, was cut off by pestilence, only two male children, under five years of age being left, who having been accustomed to see the monks, and administer to them, wept because they did not see them as usual. Ananda in order that they might be retained in the right way, admitted them before they were of the prescribed age. When he mentioned the case to Buddha, the Muni enquired if they were able to drive away the crows, and when he was told that they were, he assembled the monks and said,

"Monks, I permit children under five years of age to be admitted, if they be able to drive away the crows."

The first Upánanda had two novices, who, living together, committed sin; but when the circumstance became known, Buddha decreed:

"Monks, two novices shall not be under one person. He who receives two novices is guilty of the first offence."

When Sákya Muni had spent a whole year in Rajagaha, the inhabitants complained that the place was darkened with the number of priests. Upon this being reported to Buddha, he determined to visit another place, Ḍakkhinigiri, and sent Ananda to inform the monks, that as many of them as were inclined might accompany him. They replied, that the Muni had commanded them to remain near their superiors and preceptors ten years. "If they go," they said, "we will accompany them; otherwise we cannot go." In consequence of this the Muni had but few attendants; and upon his return he decreed:

"Monks, I decree, that fluent-speaking and well-informed monks shall remain as pupils five years. They who are not fluent-speaking shall remain as pupils as long as they live"

The qualifications requisite to free a monk of five years' standing are: that he be reverent and modest in his deportment, diligent, intelligent, free from ecclesiastical censure, orthodox, learned, wise, well acquainted with the ecclesiastical laws, and able distinctly, clearly, and in proper order, to recite the two Prátimókshas.

The Muni having resided in Rajagaha as long as he thought proper, left the place to visit his native city, Kapilavastu; and on arriving there he took up his abode at Nigrôdha grove. The mother of Ráhula, who was the wife of Buddha, before he became a monk, said to her son, "Your father is come: go and ask for your inheritance." Then the prince went to Buddha, and, standing before him, said, "Pleasant is your shadow, Muni." Buddha then rose from his seat, and departed; but Ráhula followed him, saying, "Monk, give me my inheritance! Monk, give me my inheritance!" Then Buddha called one of his two principal monks, Sáriputta, and said, "Sáriputta, admit prince Ráhula to profession." The monk asked in what manner it should be done; upon which Buddha assembled the monks and said:

"Monks, I ordain that a novice shall be admitted by thrice repeating the sarana. And thus shall he be admitted: First, let the head and beard be shaved, yellow robes put on him, and one shoulder being bared, let him worship the feet of the monks, and kneeling down with joined hands say, 'I take refuge in Buddha, I take refuge in the Dharma, I take refuge in the Sangha.' A second time, 'I take refuge in Buddha, &c.' A third time, 'I take refuge in Buddha, &c.' I direct, monks, that by thus thrice repeating the sarana, a novice shall be admitted."

The prince Ráhula was thus received, but his grandfather, Suddhôdana, came to Buddha, and said that he had experienced much sorrow when he himself (Gotama, afterwards Buddha) became a monk; that this was much increased when Ananda received profession, and that the reception of Ráhula, whom he loved with the most tender affection, was like tearing off the skin, and crushing the bones and marrow; and requested that in future no person should be admitted unless he had first obtained the consent of his parents. Buddha consoled his father by explaining the Dharma to him; and when he had retired, he assembled the monks and said:

"Monks, no person should be received by you, who has not previously obtained the consent of his parents. He who receives him is guilty of the first offence."

Afterwards Buddha left Kapilavastu, and went to live at Sáwatti. At that time a family who ministered to Sáriputta, brought one of their sons to him, and requested that he would receive him as a novice. Sáriputta, although desirous to meet their wishes, remembered that Buddha had prohibited any priest from having more than one novice under his charge, and he already had Ráhula. He stated the circumstance to Buddha, who decreed:

"I permit, monks, that an eloquent and well-informed monk may have two novices under his care, or as many as he can advise and instruct."

The novices then desired to know what precepts they were to observe, when Buddha decreed:

"I direct, monks, that novices shall be taught the ten precepts, and obey them. To abstain from destroying life; to abstain from theft; to abstain from incontinence; to abstain from lying; to abstain from intoxicating liquors; to abstain from taking food after mid-day, from dancing, singing, playing on musical instruments, and theatrical representations; from the use of flowers, garlands, perfumes, and cosmetics; from the use of high or large couches; and from receiving gold or silver. I direct, monks, that the novices shall be taught these ten precepts, and be subject to them."

Some sámanéros became careless, and disrespectful, and disobedient, to the older monks. This being reported to Buddha he decreed:

"Monks, I direct that novices guilty of the five acts following shall be subject to penal discipline (*danda kamman*): viz., if they strive to diminish the prosperity of the monks, to render them uncomfortable, to remove them from their dwellings, if they speak insolently and abusively to the monks, or if they excite dissentions between monks; I direct, monks, that for any of these five offences, a novice shall be placed under penal discipline.

CHAPTER III.

THE ISSUES OF LIFE.*

I. THE DEATH OF BUDDHA.

The circumstances immediately preceding the death of Sákya Muni are related at length in the three pitakas, as are those connected with the death of Jesus Christ in the four gospels. The Buddhist story professes to be related by Ananda, as an eye-witness; St. John had the same privilege, and was the author of the fourth of the synoptical gospels.

Whilst Sákya Muni resided at Rajagaha, he commanded the priests to be collected together in the Hall of Assembly; and then seated on his throne, he delivered an address, informing them that so long as they abstained from establishing that which had not been prescribed, or from abrogating that which had been established, and, accepting the precepts as they were laid down, should inculcate and maintain them, the Dharma would prosper. He also gave them five series of "imperishable precepts," the second of which was to the following effect: That the same prosperity would continue as long as they abstained from excessive indulgence in things allowable, and from unprofitable gossip, from an indolent (sleepy) way of existence

* The concluding chapter exists only in the rough draft of the Author, not having been fairly written out and revised by him as were the former parts of this work. It has been deciphered with some difficulty, but it is believed with accuracy. It must however be remembered that the following pages have not had the benefit of Mr. Hardy's final correction. In the first draft, the present chapter is entitled "The issues of death;" the title as given above is found in the table of contents at the beginning of the revised MS. Ed.

and from an unprofitable mode of life, and did not evade meeting together in the (Sangha) congregation, shunned the society and friendship of the sinful, and were not discouraged from the pursuit of arhathood by having met with some trifling impediments. After this, he retired to one of the royal gardens not far distant, and thence went in order to Nálanda, Pátali, Kóti, Nádiká, and Wésáli. At Wésáli he took up his residence in a mango garden belonging to the courtezan Ambapáli, who requested him to accept a repast she would on the next day prepare for him and his attendant monks. This invitation he accepted, and delivered a discourse, confirming her in the faith, comforting her, and making her steadfastly confide therein. On her return to the city she met the rulers of Wésáli, but her suite compelled them to make way for her, and she refused to listen to their entreaty to resign to them the honour of entertaining Buddha on the next day; and though they applied to the Muni himself, he adhered to the promise he had given to the courtezan, who presented the garden as an alms offering to him and the Sangha.

He then went from Wésáli to Bélugámakó, where he called his disciples together, and told them that they were to keep the festival of Wass in the different villages around, to which they might have been invited, he himself intending to keep it where he then was. But he was now attacked by a severe illness, and had to endure much agony. He however retained his mental faculties and self-possession, and thought thus: "It would be unworthy of me were I to enter nirwána without assembling those who have assisted me, and without having spoken to the monks. It is indispensable that I should submit to this trial with fortitude, maintaining my profession as to the transitory matters of this life." From this sickness the Muni partially recovered, and was able to sit up in the pulpit. The monks expressed the hope that they might receive further instruction from him; and he gave them an assurance that he would not, like other teachers, withhold anything from them, announcing at the same time, that he could not survive the infirmities under which he then laboured, and that his career was drawing to a close. After going on moving through Wésáli in search of alms, he repaired for his noonday rest to the tope Chápála and made known that it was in the power of any supreme Buddha to prolong his existence for an age, if, whilst sojourning in this or other topes that he named, he was duly entreated thereto. Mára prevented Ananda from comprehending this saying, though repeated twice, or he would have made it with all earnestness, and when he discovered that he had allowed so golden an opportunity to pass by without improvement he retired to the foot of a tree disconcerted. Mára then seated himself by the side of the Muni, and said, "Vouchsafe to realize nirvána now, Muni; this is the appointed time for it; it has been so declared by thee on a former occasion;" (he had said at the foot of the bô-tree that he would continue his mission until the Dharma had been perfectly established.) The Muni said that his attainment of nirvána would be in three months, and announcing that he had resigned all connection with this transitory state of existence, he chanted this stanza: "Having voluntarily overcome his desire for this life, the Muni has vouchsafed to relinquish all that is transitory, connected either with his human or divine essence, casting existence from him as a victorious combatant who divests himself of his armour." This statement appears to be inconsistent with what is said of the spiritual attainments of the Muni at the time he received perfect illumination at the foot of the bô-tree; but it is regarded as marking an important era in his acquirement of the powers that led towards final emancipation, as it is one of six great occasions when the earth is said to have quaked, to do him honour, or to mark some step in his progress towards the goal at which he aimed.

On the announcement of the renunciation being made of all connection with transitory existence, when it is said that there was an earthquake, Ananda inquiring what were the causes of earthquakes, the Sákya stated eight reasons, all of which are miraculous except the first which is contrary to fact. He said that the great earth rests on water—the water being sustained by wind, and the wind by air—and "when a storm prevails a natural earthquake is produced." Ananda now interfered, and requested the Muni to live an age, "for the happiness of multitudes, out of compassion for the world and for the welfare of all beings divine and human." But the Muni said that the time was now passed for this entreaty to be made, and somewhat disingenuously attached blame to his attendant, because he had not made it when it might have been of some avail, and requested, that as he was to die in three months, he might not be further afflicted by unavailing importunity. Then addressing himself to the assembly of monks,* he told them not to be self-opinionated nor hasty in adopting the opinions of other monks; but if any such doctrines were set forth, to examine them dispassionately, with reference to his own Dharma; if they agreed with it, they were to adopt them, if not, they were to be rejected.

* Journ R. A. S. No 84, p. 1003.

On visiting the mango grove belonging to a smith named Chunda, and consenting to receive from him a repast, he said to his host, "Chunda, if any pork is to be dressed by thee (for the occasion) serve to me only, and let the monks have other provisions." This charge he repeated, and said that if any pork was left it was to be buried, under the plea that there was no other being in the universe who could digest it if he partook of it. The promise was given that his orders should be strictly obeyed. Soon afterwards he was attacked by a violent fit of dysentery, but he succeeded in reaching the city of Kusinári. Ananda entreated him to go to a spot a little higher up the Kukuttha river, as the water near the place where he was had been fouled by the passing of five hundred carts; but by a miracle he rendered it perfectly clear, and the owner of the carts bestowed in alms two pieces of cloth of gold, one to Buddha and one to Ananda; these were thrown around him by his attendant, as his sufferings from the disease were great. The Muni then entered the stream, bathed in it, and drank of the water; and when he reached the opposite bank, proceeded to another mango grove; when he enjoined Ananda to relieve the mind of the goldsmith from all apprehension about his death, and to tell him of the reward he would receive for that act of charity and faith. He then repaired to a grove of sal-trees, below two of which he requested Ananda to prepare his bed, placing his head to the north; on which he lay down on his left side. Flowers in the grove, though it was not the time for their blooming, descended spontaneously on his head, celestial musicians that had assembled made the air ring with the music of the heavens, and flowers of various kinds were showered down upon him from above in his last hours; but he said on noticing it, that the observance of the Dharma would be a recognition of him equally acceptable. He requested one of his disciples, Upawánó, who was fanning him to retire: and when Ananda asked the reason, he said that the deities of ten thousand worlds were hovering in the air, and lamenting his death, and that they ought not to be prevented from seeing him by the body of the disciple being interposed between him and them. Ananda retired to weep in private, but the Muni sent for him, and comforted him by expressing approbation of his past conduct, and giving him an assurance that he would shortly attain arhathood. He was directed to inform the Mallawa princes of Kusinári that in the last watch of that night he would attain nirwána, and that he would wish them to be present. On hearing this, there was great lamentation throughout the city; and as the people attended in such numbers that they could not individually pay reverence to the dying sage, Ananda divided them into sections, according to their tribes; and the members of each tribe bowed down at the same time, with their hands raised over their heads, he calling out, "Muni, such a tribe, with their sons, daughters, and followers are bowing down at the feet of Bhagawá with uplifted hands." But Buddha made no reply, though he afterwards held a conversation with Subhadra, one of his disciples, by which his doubts were removed, and he was admitted to arhathood, he being the last person to whom the privilege was personally vouchsafed by the Muni. He gave advice to his monks as to the manner in which they were henceforth to address each other, the younger monks being respectful to the elder; and he then asked whether they had any doubts as to the Dharma or its meaning, and if so they were now to declare them, that they might not reproach themselves afterwards by saying, "When the Muni was present with us we lost the opportunity he gave us of making personal enquiry from him." But on on being thus addressed they remained silent; and when exhorted a second and a third time, they still remained silent. They were told if it was out of reverence for their master that they abstained from making inquiry, they were to commission one of their number to speak for the rest, but still they remained silent as before. Ananda said, "This is wonderful, not in any one monk is there any doubt or want of comprehension;" when Buddha informed him that he could see with his divine eyes that the conclusion of his attendant was true. The last words that he said were: "Transitory things are perishable; without delay address yourselves for the reception of nirvána." He then became absorbed in the exercise of profound meditation, ascending step by step through its various stages; after which he descended, and between the fourth and fifth stage, he expired, "in the full possession of his mental faculties, like the extinction of the flame of a lamp."

We can scarcely read this record without some emotion, though conscious that it is a fiction; and the fictitiousness of its character adds to our regret, as we are called upon to regard it as presenting the most hopeful circumstances that men educated in his system can imagine concerning the manner of his death. A venerable man, of most irreproachable conduct, after essaying to instruct the world in the most important problems of human thought, for the long space of forty-five years, retires to a grove of trees, that he may die in the midst of his disciples and followers. We may reject the music of the heavenly choristers, and the floral shower poured down from celestial hands, and confine ourselves to the simple record of the old man's last hours. There are the old evidences of the spirit of kindness that had ever marked all his course, in the message he sent to the smith, the words he spoke to the monks, and his tender sympathy with his attendant, Ananda; but as a severe disease racks his body, though it leaves his mind still collected, there is no expression of hope for the future. To him there is to be no future; according to his own teaching, "life's fitful fever" is over; his mortal will put on no immortality; the mind that had silenced so many reasonings is now to become as though it had never been, and to be nothing, like the last wave of the pebble that dies away on the surface of the pleasant lake, or the last flicker of the flame that had shone from the bright lamp the oil of which is now expended. As his followers can scarcely hope to rise to a higher state of privilege than their founder, we are prepared to learn that myriads of his disciples die without any bright ray to gild their pathway to the gates of death.

II. THE DEATH OF CHRIST.

There was one thing that so exclusively occupied the mind of the apostle Paul, and was so prominent a subject in all his instructions, that he could say "we preach Christ crucified; to the Jews a stumbling-block and to the Greeks foolishness, but to those which are called Christ the power of God and the wisdom of God." This is not an isolated instance in the record of the lessons received by the members of the Church of God. In the prophets, not only the general features in the character of Jesus are presented, but the most minute circumstances are foretold connected with His death and burial. In the conversations He held with His disciples, His own thoughts seemed continually to revert to the same event; and so much importance did He attach to it, that when He had spoken of its approach, and Peter had remonstrated with Him saying, "Be it far from Thee, Lord; this shall not be to Thee," He replied, with unwonted earnestness, that the apostle was "an offence to Him, as he savoured not the things that are of God, but those that are of men;" thus showing that he was unconsciously putting forth a suggestion of Satan in seeking to make Him reluctant to endure the sufferings that were before Him. Only once were beings permitted to come from the other world and converse with Him, but in the short space occupied by their conversation, they "spake of the decease He would accomplish at Jerusalem." On all other occasions nature seemed unheedful of the circumstance that Christ was present, but at His death we are told that "the veil of the temple was rent in twain." (Matt. xxvii. 50.) Even in heaven there is an attention to the same subject; it is first among the celestial hosts as among the members of the Church on earth. In preparing us for the sight of Christ's power and majesty, the apostle John says, "Unto Him that loved us, aud washed us from our sins in His own blood, and hath made us kings and priests unto God and His Father, to Him be glory and dominion for ever and ever. Amen." (Rev. i. 5.) The many angels round about the Throne, and the beasts, and the elders, the number of them being ten thousand times ten thousand, and thousands of thousands, sing with a loud voice, "Worthy is the Lamb." (Rev. v. 12.) And again they cry, "Blessing and honour, and glory and power, be unto Him that sitteth upon the throne and unto the Lamb for ever and ever." (Rev. v. 13.) Yet in the same book we have one of those worshipping angels saying unto John who had fallen down before his feet to worship him, "See that thou do it not: for I am thy fellow servant, and of thy brethren the prophets, and of those that keep the sayings of this book: worship God." (Rev. xxii. 8.) Then, upon the testimony of the angels, Jesus is not a fellow servant; not one among even the most exalted of the holy followers of the prophets. Any one of those it would have been wrong to worship; but Jesus was worthy, as He sat upon the throne of God, and "was God."

The great mystery constantly meets us, "God manifested in the flesh:" and in all instances which we have recorded, the principal fact to which reference is made, is not so much to the incarnation as to the redemption by blood, His agony and death. The only sacrament He ordained to be continually repeated was instituted only a short time before the death struggle had commenced, and the bread that was to be eaten and the wine to be drunk, were appointed as emblems of His wounded and bleeding body, and the wine was called the blood of the new Testament, which is shed for many for the remission of sins. Unless the words of Christ were figurative, if He held in His hand parts of His own body, He being yet alive, the doctrine of the Church cannot be true that "He was proper man, of human flesh subsisting," and the guilty sinner is left without a sufficient atonement for his iniquities. The safety of the Church is placed in peril by those who hold the corporal presence in the celebration of this rite or who would nullify the whole meaning of Christ's redemption by daring to say, "Our hands have touched God."

It is supposed that the anointing of the Lord "for His burial" was on the first of the month of April, or on the 9th of Nisan. When Christ said, "against the day of my burying hath she kept this;" the near approach of the hour of the great Sacrifice was made known. The next day was the time appointed for the separation of the paschal lamb, when Christ the true Passover saw Jerusalem and entered in triumph, after the multitude had cried out, "Hosanna to the Son of David." so that the whole city was said to be moved and alarmed. It was on the same day that he wept over Jerusalem, now to be left desolate, and the same day the fig tree was withered. The Jews were now more anxious than ever to draw Him into some utterance upon which they might lay hold, and have a pretext for presenting Him before the tribunals of the land, either secular or ecclesiastical; but, in both of the questions they asked from him, and in the one about the payment of money, and in the question He asked from them, when He said "What think ye of Christ," they were foiled by their own weapons, and the intended accusation was made to recoil upon their own heads. In the temple there was a reassertion of the terrible truth, first spoken among his tears and re-echoed by the seared fig-tree, when he said, "O Jerusalem, Jerusalem, thou that killest the prophets and stonest them which are sent unto thee, how often would I have gathered thy children together, even as a hen gathereth her chickens under her wings, and ye would not! Behold your house is left unto you desolate." On Wednesday, the 5th, the powers of hell entered into a confederacy with earth, and "the devil put into the heart of Judas Iscariot, Simon's son, to betray Him." Thursday, the 6th, was the "first day of unleavened bread," when the passover was prepared by the disciples, and Jesus announced that one of His disciples would betray Him. Of Judas, who had already sold himself to the evil one, we are told that "Satan now entered into him." There was now the institution of the Lord's Supper, the great purpose of which was to "shew forth the Lord's death till He come." The agony of the garden soon followed, in the midst of which Jesus gently and lovingly apologized for the sleeping of the disciples by saying, "The spirit is willing, but the flesh is weak;" and when the ground upon which he knelt was softened with drops of His own blood that had fallen in that hour of darkness, His soul was sorrowful unto death. He said, "Father, Thy will be done!" These were evidences of Christ's majesty in the midst of all the indignities He was made to suffer at the hands of wicked men.

When Jesus said to the men who entered the garden to seize His person, "I am He," they went backwards and fell to the ground. There appeared an angel from heaven, strengthening Him. To Peter He said, "Thinkest thou that I cannot now pray to My Father, and He shall presently give me more than twelve legions of angels?" Throughout the entire period of these unexampled trials we have proof that the ingratitude of men had not changed, in any degree, the outflowing of His love towards the world he had come to redeem. With the highest displays of the love of the Son of God there are connected the saddest evidences of the meanness and hard-heartedness of men. "Of the people there are none with me." We might ask, Where are the lepers whom He cleansed; the blind to whom He gave sight; the dumb whose tongues He had unloosed; the multitudes whom He had fed in the wilderness; relations and friends, at least, of those of the three, whom He had raised from the dead? We sometimes say that women were the last at the cross and the first at the sepulchre. But this is not their only honour. The wife of Pilate entreated the governor on His behalf, and the women of Jerusalem followed Him, bewailing Him and lamenting Him. The only voices uplifted in His behalf, expressing grief for His suffering, were those of women. The disciples all forsook Him and fled. By one disciple He was betrayed, by another denied. The indignities He had to suffer from the servants and the soldiers were so great, and of such a nature, that we wonder the arm was not paralyzed when uplifted to strike, and they themselves not smitten dead in the act. But He came not to destroy man's life but to save. Even His last moments were disturbed by the railing and insults of the people, who said, wagging their heads, "Thou that destroyest the temple and buildest it in three days, save Thyself." Those who came with Judas are still addressed in words of kindness. To His captors He said, "If ye seek me, let these (my unfaithful disciples) go their way." He healed Malchus who had come with the rest to bind Him He turned to Peter in the act of transgression, with the old look of compassion and love, in a manner that brought him to repentance. To the malefactor who had previously reviled Him, He said, "To-day shalt thou be with Me in Paradise." Upon the cross He prayed for His murderers, "Father, forgive them, for they know not what they do." To the very last never man loved like this Man! "When Jesus saw His mother, and the disciple standing by, whom He loved, He said unto His mother, Woman behold thy son! Then said He to the disciple, Behold thy mother! And from that hour that disciple took her to his own house."

When all had been accomplished, the example was perfect, and the work of redemption complete, Jesus said, "Father, into Thy hands I commend My spirit; And having said this, He bowed His head and gave up the ghost." We cannot follow His glorified spirit into the other world, as we have been able to trace His steps from the manger to the sepulchre, but a little we are permitted to know by inference and immediate revelation.

The death of Christ was not, as with the Muni, the end of existence; it was the beginning of a more glorious life in which he was to abide in bliss, "world without end, for ever and ever."

Turning from Buddha to Christ is like passing away from the deep darkness to the most intense light. When He said, "It is finished," it was not despairingly as the Muni would have said it, but in hope, the most exultant and joyful. The last pain had been endured, the last drop of the bitter cup had been drunk, the last moment of oppression from the crushing weight of the world's guilt was about to pass away. The last onslaught of Satan had been triumphantly met: "for this Man after He had offered one sacrifice for sins for ever, sat down at the right hand of God, from henceforth expecting, till His enemies be made His footstool." Heb. x. 12.